The earl[illegible] d

And Griqualand Eas[illegible]

William Dower

Alpha Editions

This edition published in 2019

ISBN : 9789353609139

Design and Setting By
Alpha Editions
email - alphaedis@gmail.com

THE

EARLY ANNALS

OF

KOKSTAD

AND

GRIQUALAND EAST.

—BY—

REV. WILLIAM DOWER,

OF

PORT ELIZABETH.

PRINTED BY JAS. KEMSLEY & Co.,

PORT ELIZABETH.

1902.

CHAPTER I.

During a visit recently paid to the rising town of Kokstad, my attention was more than once called to the fact that of those who took part in the founding of the town 30 years ago, I only am left. The Rev. William Murray, who subsequently became, and has continued till now, to be closely associated with the history of the town, left the district immediately afte the site had been fixed on, and did not return till 11 years thereafter. Adam Kok, the Griqua Chief, after whom the town was named, Charles Brisley, his Secreta'y, Edward Barker, who filled the position of Surveyor, and every member of the old Heemraad or Privy Council has passed away. The last of the two men who held office, as Magistrate, from 1869 to 1872, while the town was taking shape—the late Lodowijk Kok, of somewhat painful memory to the present generation—has quite recently also deceased More than one of the citizens suggested that I should use some leisure moments in compiling reminiscences of the early days of the Township. The suggestion in some instances took the stronger form of an urgent request. There is always a wonderful fascination around the beginning of things. The dwellers in a city or even the merest hamlet are curious to know when, how, by whose thought and toil it came originally to have a local habitation and a name. I do not mean to say that there are not Griquas still living who have knowledge of these things. Members of the old Griqua Volksraad and Field-cornets of Wards are still to be seen walking the streets of Kokstad, shorn, of course, of their authority and dignity, and mourning the loss of their emoluments. Some of these men have, or had, wondrous gifts of speech. Indeed, if it comes to speaking on any subject of which they think they have a little knowledge, I am afraid the best of us would have to take a back seat; but apart from this facile loquacity, I am not aware that any of them has shown any literary fitness to record the early annals of a nascent city.

I lay no claim to special literary qualifications for such a work, but I am moved to attempt it by the clinching remark of my old friend, T. Coulter, Esq., the Mayor of Kokstad, when he said to me, "Well, if you cannot, or will not place on record the story of the early settlement of this town, then most of the facts will die with you." I accept that challenge. What may come of my attempt remains to be seen.

I propose to bring these Annals down to the termination of the Basuto War. After that, it becomes "modern history," and the events are well known to the present inhabitants, and besides are recorded in the files of the local paper.

The story of the founding of the town of Kokstad is inseparably linked with the story of the settlement of the Griquas in East Griqualand or Nomansland, or, as the, Griquas first called it NEW GRIQUALAND. That, again, cannot be rightly understood without some knowledge of their previous history, and especially their political status in the country, which is now the Orange River Colony. That, again, leads to questions as to their antecedents. Who are the Griquas? Whence came they? The physique of the pure Griqua, and especially the features, show him to belong to the Hottentot, not to the Kaffir race.

CHAPTER II.

When Europeans first landed in Table Bay, there was a considerable variety of Hottentot tribes living in different parts of the country, such as the Damaqua, Gonaqua, Inqua, Hessequa, Damaqua, and Grigriqua. Memorials of these tribes remain among us in the names of districts and places.

The Grigriquas were located along the coast, in the neighbourhood of what is now the District of Malmesbury. As the white man pushed northwards, he displaced the Grigriquas, who kept moving on until they crossed the Orange River. They then moved eastwards, attracted by the rich lands and flowing fountains in the country, now known as Griqualand West. There they settled down undisturbed, living on the proceeds of the chase, and the milk of their cattle. They are described in 1800 as "a herd of wandering and naked savages subsisting by plunder and the chase. Their bodies were daubed with red paint, their heads loaded with grease and shinny powder, with no covering, but the filthy kaross over their shoulders, without knowledge, without morals or any traces of civilization, they were wholly abandoned to witch-craft, drunkenness and licentiousness." They cultivated no ground, they built only the *maantje* house—a slight basket frame of wattles, covered with rush-mats, which could be erected or taken down by the wife, while the man boiled the kettle. When I visited the Griquas at the Mount Currie

Laager first in 1869, one of these *maantje* huts was still in use. The owner, an old widow, declined to live in any of the new fangled square houses. She said the old is better, and she stuck to it, and died in it.

Two agencies co operated to introduce the elements of civilization. First, Missionary Agency, commenced about 1800, and next, the large influx of escaped slaves from the Colony. These brought with them not only a considerable admixture of European blood, but such rudiments of civilization as they had acquired from their Dutch masters. Griqualand, as we may call it, became, as the years passed on, to the slaves from the Colony, a sort of Canada, a refuge from the storm, a covert from the tempest, a land of liberty. These half-caste slaves had something of the energy and self-reliance and "go" of their European fathers, while the colour inherited from their slave mothers qualified them for what Burgher rights existed among the Griquas. As time went on, the three elements, Griqua, slave, and half-caste freely intermingled, producing the exceedingly mixed race we now see.

At first, the pure Griquas were the wealthier and more numerous, and constituted the nobility of the tribe. All the others were "*Sommar mensche*," only ordinary mortals. They also gave a name to the whole—a name they have retained after the pure Griqua has almost become extinct. The dropping of the reduplication in the tribal name is easily accounted for, just as we abreviate all long common names. Among the Dutch of the Colony, they were long known as "*The Bastards*," a descriptive title given with greater regard to fact than to courtesy.

Some time in the thirties the tribe divided, and each half had its elected chief. Waterboer, with one half, chiefly pure Griquas, settled around Griquatown. Adam Kok, or "Dam" Kok, as he was familiarly called, with the other half, chiefly half-casts, settled between the Modder and the Orange Rivers, with the Caledon for an eastern boundary, and the line which now divides the Orange River Colony from Griqualand West as his western border. Here they founded the town of Philipolis, calling it after the late Dr. Philip of Cape Town.

The genealogy of the Kok family is about as perplexing to those who have neither time nor inclination to investigate it as that of the Herod family of Jewish history. Considering how various important questions of territorial rights to some of the most valuable spots of this globe of ours, hinged on the relationships, status, and actions of different members of this family, and how these questions forced them from obscurity into prominence in South African history, it will not be amiss here to append a brief genealogical statement:—

ADAM KOK I,—Born about 1710. He, according to

one tradition, was cook to a Dutch Governor in Cape Town, according to another tradition, he was cook on board a Dutch East Indiaman and escaped from the service, made his way north, joined the Griquas, and by his force of character, skill, and resourcefulness gained the suffrages of the people, and became chief. He held a staff of office under the Dutch Governor, and died during the closing days of the century, leaving a large family.

CORNELIUS KOK (old), succeeded Adam 1st.—He travelled to Cape Town to surrender his hereditary staff of office and get an English one. He also left a large family.

ADAM KOK II.—"Dam" Kok succeeded Cornelius. He founded the town of Philipolis about 1825, and was recognised by the Cape Governor as occupying a position independent of Waterboer on the west. Died 1837.

ABRAHAM KOK—"Dam's" eldest son, — succeeded to the chieftainship, but the people would have none of him, and after some disturbance they elected his brother, Adam, who, on the death of Abraham, married the widow and fathered the three daughters.

ADAM KOK III.—This is the Kok who by the treaties of '43 '46 and '48 was recognised as a sovereign prince. This is the man who authorized the sale of the residuary estate of the Griqua Government in 1862, on which sale the Orange Free State founded its claim to the Diamond Fields. This is the Adam Kok who trekked from Philipolis to *Nomansland*, and founded the town of Kokstad there.

One other Kok deserves a passing notice. CORNELIUS KOK (the younger).—He was a brother of "Dam" Kok, son of old Cornelius, uncle to Adam 3rd. The claims of the Orange Free State to the ownership of the Diamond Fields were founded on the assumptions:—

1. That C. Kok was an independent chief and owner of the lands on which diamonds were discovered.
2. That Adam Kok, his nephew, was his heir;
3. That Adam Kok sold the land to the Orange Free State.

All these assumptions were disproved.

Under Adam Kok 2nd, the people prospered. They gave up their nomadic habits; divided their country into farms; had flocks of cattle, sheep and horses, and began to cultivate the soil, enclose lands, and build houses. A church and school had been established, and a vigorous Christian settlement had arisen when the last Adam Kok succeeded to the chieftainship.

CHAPTER III.

Early in the forties, the British Colonial policy towards the coloured tribes was to avoid trouble as far as possible by granting to them a limited independence. The Governors

Napier and Maitland, under instructions, concluded treaties with native chiefs. beginning with Waterboer on the west, and comprehending those whose territories extended to the Drakensburg and on to the Indian Ocean. By these treaties the sovereignty of the various chiefs—*Waterboer, Kok, Moshesh*, and *Faku*, was recognised, and guaranteed under the Queen's authority. The chiefs attained at once the dignity of sovereign potentates, the Queen's allies, and confederates. This became the beginning of sorrows for South Africa. For certain annual payments the British Government promised supplies of powder and protection against all comers. Kok was now bound to guard his boundary conterminous with the Colony against incursions from the regions beyond. In the cases of Waterboer and Kok, especially the latter, these treaties became the seed from which the prolific crop of political complications arose which kept our diplomatists and governors busy during the years which followed on the discovery of diamonds on the imperfectly defined boundary between the territories of the two. Adam Kok issued individual titles to his burghers for their farms. Morally, the English Government became bound to recognise the validity of these titles when political relations came to be rearranged. We shall find, however, that it failed to do so. From 1840 onwards, the Emigrant farmers began to cross the Orange River. They envied the excellent pasture lands, the unfailing fountains and agricultural holdings of the Griquas. They had been trained from childhood to look on men of colour as only fit to be menials, and now to see them land-owners, prosperous, independent, free, was offensive—almost unbearable.

The Griqua law forbade the sale of a Griqua farm to a white man. Both Dutch and Griqua practically evaded the law by leasing for a term of years. The owner took payment from the lessee often for the whole term of the lease at once. In such cases, especially when the lease was a long one, the tenant was apt to forget that he was only a tenant, and not owner. To the proprietor the only tangible evidence of his ownership during the lease was the possession of a dirty, generally dilapidated paper declaring in bad Dutch that A.B. was first applicant for such and such a farm, which might or might not be defined as to extent and boundaries. The Dutch lessee became nominally a Griqua subject. The European tenants chafed under Griqua rule, and incessant squabbles arose. The Imperial Government claimed the emigrant farmers as British subjects still amenable to British authority, while the Griquas who were her allies, she was bound to protect; hence inevitable trouble. By the Maitland treaty, the country of Kok was devided into *alienable* and *inalienable*. The distinction was better expressed in the Dutch "*huurbaar*" and "*onhuurbaar*." In the former, the northern part, owners might lease for any period not exceeding 40 years. In the latter, there could be neither lease nor sale.

In 1848, after the battle of *Boom Plaats*, which was fought largely in defence of Griqua rights, another treaty was drawn by the redoubtable Sir Harry Smith. By this treaty 42 farms were ceded to the Government in perpetuity, and certain *perpetual* payments secured to the chief and the owners of these farms. The provisions of the treaty were, beyond all doubt, distasteful to the Griquas. Right or wrong, the Governor believed that the Treaty was necessary for the future peace of the country, and he insisted on the Griqua chief accepting it. When he hesitated, the Governor lost his temper, and made use of some strong language, even threatening to hang the chief on the beams of the house if he did not sign it. Under this intimidation, Kok signed the Treaty. Against the matter and the manner of it Kok never ceased to protest till the day of his death. That substantial injury and injustice was done is now generally admitted. Not even the entangled and complicated interests which had arisen justified it. It was the soldiers' rough way of cutting the knot That treaty created a grievance which was never forgotten. Every old resident in Kokstad is familar with the ceaseless growl about the "*Vertig jaar's geld.*" Forty two farms were ceded; the owners received £100 amongst them. The chief was to receive £200. The chief dies without an heir to the succession. The country is annexed. As a matter of grace, £100 is continued to his widow. When she dies this grant lapses. As time goes on, there is a gradual reduction by death of the number of the 42 participants. Those who live draw their share and their heirs after them, if they have any, and can prove their right. Some deceased shareholders have left scores of heirs. Questions of marriage, legitimacy, testamentary disposition, native law, all come in, till the case bristles with difficulties. The lawyer smiles as he contemplates the prospect of a fine harvest of costs in such a case. The divided share would in some cases give a few pence to each heir. The ultimate issue will be that either there will be none to draw, or so many that the available amount would only be sufficient to pay the stamps on the receipts How to deal with this, has taxed the wits of successive Missionaries, Magistrates, and Cabinet Ministers. To a suspicious people, already sore over real or imaginary wrongs, and unable to comprehend the legal difficulties in the way of a final settlement, all this wears the aspect of studied injustice. Whether Government will ever be persuaded to deal with the difficulty and terminate it, remains to be seen. It is there to this day.

CHAPTER IV.

In 1848 Great Britain reversed the *"leave alone"* policy, and proclaimed her Sovereignty over the whole territory between the Orange and the Vaal, and established a firm government at Bloemfontein.

The proclamation failed sufficiently to define the position of Adam Kok and his little state. Were they now British subjects or not? Was the old treaty abrogated or not? No one could tell.

Then six years thereafter, in 1854, Britain again reverted to the "scuttle" policy. Sir George Clerk handed back to the Emigrant Boers the country which is now the O.R. Colony. Again there was the same uncertainty as to Kok's position. He and his Raad urged the home government to define his position. He urged in vain. Sir George Clerk in the Queen's name declared in the Bloemfontein Convention that treaty obligations existed between Her Majesty and Adam Kok, while almost simultaneously, Imperial officers declared the Treaties abrogated.

A very serious practical difficulty now arose. Many farms belonging to Griquas were leased to Boers. The leases were not expired, and Great Britain by the Bloemfontein Convention sought once and for all to wash her hands of all responsibilities north of the Orange River. This was an integral part of the new Convention. Sir George Clerk tried hard to negotiate the purchase of these farms with the unexpired leases, and even sent a Commissioner to Philipolis with £11,000 cash. Every proposal to purchase or compensate for the cession of these farms *was accompanied with the condition that the old Griqua law prohibiting the sale of farms within Kok's boundary should be abrogated.* The large sum was spread out on the table before the eyes of Kok and his Councillors along with the new treaty ready for signature. They, the Griquas, declared themselves ready to negotiate for the sale in order to avoid complications, but declined to change the prohibitory law. The negotiations ended, and the money went back to Bloemfontein. Then followed, a most shameful piece of political chicanery. As these leases of the hired farms expired, the Griqua owners each in turn claimed his property. He was referred to the Republican Government at Bloemfontein, which had in the meantime issued Free State titles in favour of the Boer tenant. The Government at Bloemfontein politely referred them to the British Government which had "*given them the country.*" The British Government as good as said "*We have now no interests or responsibilities north of the Orange River.*" The Boer occupant closed the controversy by the pious remark: "Ja vriendje Klaas zalig is de bezitter." The Griqua owner put the old futile "*Request*" away in his "kist" with the remark "Mensche het is zwaar als magt eens regt wordt." I have had in my hand Griqua titles to valuable farms in the Orange Free State which thus passed into possession of the Orange Free State Boers, for which the Griqua proprietor never received one shilling. This was not even the worst part of the proceeding. A Secret Deed was drawn up, but *not published.* By its terms it was provided that from that date every farm leased to a European by a Griqua or subject of Adam Kok, in any part of his country, *became* ipso facto, *part and parcel of the new Republic.*

During the three succeeding years every inducement was offered to the Griquas to sell. In defiance of their own law, a perfect mania for selling seized them, such as many of us witnessed in Kokstad after 1874. The first effect was that in a short time adjoining farms acknowledged separate jurisdictions, according as they belonged to Griqua or Boer. The Boer residing in Kok's country defied the summons and authority of the Griqua law officer, because he had bought the farm, and it was now Free State. The Griqua repudiated the authority claimed by the Government at Bloemfontein. Then followed mutual recrimination, incessant strife and bickerings, a seething, weltering ferment of things, ever tending to confusion worse confounded.

In 1857 the Free State boldly published the Secret Treaty and proceeded to divide Kok's country into Wards, and appoint Field-cornets over them. The Griquas and Boers both talked of war, and began to prepare for it.

Sir George Grey was now Governor. He was distinguished for generosity, justice, and wisdom. He was the tried friend of the native peoples, but in this case his hands were tied by the terms of the Convention, "*no interests north of Orange River.*" The Boers had laid their plans with traditional slimness. The Governor dare not send a soldier or a rifle over the Orange River to the help of a people up till now the most faithful of all our native allies.

Sir George appealed to the Bloemfontein Government *ad misericordiam.* It appealed to the Convention and its appended provisions, and claimed its pound of flesh. Sir George Grey protested in his despatches against the wrong which had been done. The Home Government said: "Do anything you like, but do not spend Imperial money." Sir George was unsparing in his condemnation of all parties concerned, not excluding the Griquas, who, by selling in the teeth of their own law, had largely helped to create the impossible situation. It is well-known that the Boers at first were not disposed to accept the proffered independence. Probably what they thought was something like this: "How can a Boer independent state exist side by side with black men aping Government and claiming soverign rights—the slave of yesterday, to-day assuming the position of ruler? No, no, clear them out, or give us the chance of clearing them out, and then we are willing." Thus the clause about non-interference north of the Orange River and the secret treaty slipped into the bargain and the little State was doomed. Every bit of land a Griqua sold was then like another nail in the coffin of his cherished independence.

About 1859 the Free State sent to Adam Kok a copy of the official organ of the State with the secret treaty, and he had to face the alternative, fight or trek. One can hardly call it an alternative, for just at this time Imperial officers intimated to Kok that the old Treaty was annulled, and that no powder or ammunition could be permitted. This welded the last link of the chain that bound Kok and his people, neck and heel, at the mercy of the Orange Free State. Sir George Grey advised a general trek to pastures new, and suggested Nomansland.

These are the circumstances in Griqua and Colonial History, which culminated in the exodus to the new country.

The following extract from an article in the Cape Monthly of Dec. 1872, describes the condition of the people when the movement became necessary:—"The people were in a prosperous state, they had titles to their farms on which they had built substantial cottages and out-buildings, orchards stocked with good fruit trees, garden grounds and lands for cultivation were, in many cases, enclosed with stone walls; good stone kraals, and one or two dams were to be found on most farms. Troops of from 20 to 100 horses, about the same number of cattle, and hundreds of well bred wooled sheep were running on these farms, and many a man (Griqua) brought his 10, 20, 25 bales of wool for sale, while the shop-keepers found them as good customers for clothing, groceries, guns, saddlery, carts and furniture as any of the Boers. Of course there were poor people whose poverty was brought on by their own laziness, pride and drunkenness, They voluntary contributed £500 to £600 per annum for the purposes of religion and education amongst themselves, paying their own minister and head school master in Philipolis and school-masters in the country."

There existed a flourishing church, which in one respect set a wholesome example before the Boers. It paid its own way without aid either from the State Treasury or Mission funds. It did more, it contributed liberally to the needs of others.

The ministry of this Griqua church has been filled by men whose families have subsequently taken no mean place in the life and progress of this Colony. Anderson, Melville, Atkinson, Schreiner, Hughes, Wright, Solomon, Philip, are honoured names in South Africa. Judge Solomon and his brother, the Attorney-General elect for the Transvaal Colony, as well as their sisters were all either born or partly brought up in the old Griqua parsonage. The ex-Premier and his gifted sister, Olive Schreiner, are children of an old Griqua Missionary. Cronwright (Schreiner) is the grandson of another Griqua Missionary Livingstone practised the healing art among them in the Philipolis days. But for the troubles that preceded the Trek, Rev. John Mackenzie would probably have been one of their ministers.

CHAPTER V.

A commission of Griquas along with the Chief now visited Normansland. On the passage of the Drakensberg mountain, one of the party was accidently shot, hence the name "*Ongeluks Nek*" The commission explored the country which was pointed out to them by the late Sir Walter Currie. After him they named the mountain which up till now had borne the names "*Cockscomb*" *and* "*Bergvijftig*." The spies brought a good report of the land, and the Griquas decided to trek. The government then negotiated with Faku for the cession of the country. Much diplomacy was wasted in the vain effort on the part of the Griquas to secure exemption from the dreaded British citizenship. " Were they not a *natie*?" "A vrije volk" "Were they not the Queen's alies? &c." They appealed to the Independence and Sovereignty which had been acknowledged if not created by the Napier and Maitland Treaties. Sir George Grey would have none of it. They had to become British subjects *nolens volens*, or stay on and be swallowed up by the Boers. Meantime, preparation was made for the Trek. Farms were sold, wagons and oxen got ready, provisions laid in, church, school, and parsonage were sold. The Griqua Chief and his Council empowered their agent to dispose of the unallotted, or as we would say, Crown lands, which he did in December, 1862, selling to the O.F. State Government. This transaction, though regarded at the time as very simple and unimportant, came to be regarded as an act of no small interest in South African history. When diamonds were discovered 8 years later on the banks of the Vaal river, Waterboer, the Griqua Chief claimed that the diamondiferous lands lay within his line. The O.F. State contended that it lay on Kok's side, and that in virtue of the sale just mentioned it was theirs. Into the deed of sale had been cleverly introduced a very innocent looking clause: "*likewise that of the late Cornelius Kok.*" For the insertion of that clause no authority existed in the Power of Attorney, yet the O.F.S. persisted in their claim founded on the clause, and were prepared to fight for it. All this, however, lay in the future. More than once, as we shall see later on, this transaction formed the subject of discussion and inquiry on the slopes of Mount Currie, and in the rooms of the "Palace" in Kokstad.

These negotiations, sales, purchases, and preparations completed, the Trek began in 1861-62. It has been estimated that 2000 souls left Philipolis. The stock, large and small, amounted to over 20,000 head. Of wagons, carts, and vehicles there were about 300. They persisted in their purpose to cross the crest of the Drakensberg; this, partly that they might not endanger their independence by passing through British territory, partly to avoid grazing and watering charges. The season had proved exceptionally dry, and stock perished in large numbers, seriously impoverishing many who had been wealthy men when they started. The calvalcade rested for many months around *Hanglip* in Basuto land. The Basuto Chief was friendly disposed, and had agreed to give safe conduct. The sight, however, of all this multitude of stock was too great a strain on the good will of the Basutos. Stock disappeared rapidly and mysteriously. The Basutos got the blame for its disappearance, and probably they were not altogether innocent. Very likely they, arguing by rule of thumb justice, would say, "If the Griquas and their stock enjoy our hospitality and eat our grass and drink our nice water, it is only fair that we should have a tasting of their good mutton." After resting and waiting for the laggards, they began the famous passage over Ongeluk's Nek. It was no child's play. Every morning scores of men got to work with pick and crowbar, hammer and drills, powder and fuse to dig out a passable track on the mountain side. This continued for several weeks. Let any unprejudiced man visit the old Griqua pass over against the French Mission Station of *Pabalong*, let him follow the old track to the top and down the other side, or reverse the process and go from Hanglip to Pabalong, and let him take in the fact that the fathers and grandfathers of the mixed coloured residents in and around the Kokstad of to-day actually scaled those heights with wagons, families, and stock, and it will, or it ought to, bespeak a bit of respect for the memory of those hardy pioneers, whatever may be the feeling towards their descendants of to-day. Through that lofty rugged gate came to *Nomansland*, the first rudimentary civilization. As late as 1869, there were reports of heaps of broken wagons and carts with bleaching bones of horses and draught cattle still lying in and about the ravines along the route. It has been said that the abundance of iron from the wreckage rendered the smelting of ore among the Basutos for years unnecessary.

At last they were camped on the plain beneath. Away before them lay the rolling grass prairies with abundance of water, not in fountains only, but in rivers, pure, sweet, sparkling and unfailing, and these at every few hours trek. Timber, too, there was hiding its stately growth in the deep mountain kloof, the huge trunks below ripe for the woodman's axe, the dark foliage above adding variety to the picture. Fertile arable land was there, miles and miles of it without a stone to blunt the ploughman's share. Game, too, in abundance, big and little, tamely waiting for the hunter's rifle. For several years the lion continued still to pace at leisure the Umzimkulu flats till the report of fire-arms becoming a trifle too monotonous in his accustomed haunts, he disappeared. The eland had his home on the eastern slopes of the mountain. As late as 1875, Griquas went eland hunting, and returned with loads of biltong. Large and small game were everywhere. Then, and for long after, myriads of water fowl were to be seen all along the Umzimkulu. Surely this was a goodly land, a land full of promise and splendid possibilities. I am persuaded that there are few districts of South Africa to equal it Yet, somehow the Griquas never took to it, never believed in its fertility and pastoral qualities until it was too late. They spoke with ill-concealed contempt of its capabilities. "The grass was too long, the winter too cold, the rains too heavy, the markets too far, the money too scarce, the merchandise too dear, the Kaffirs too "parmantig." Some folk are never satisfied. They want to have the first fruits every month, the living green, the never-withering flowers on this side of the better land. We knew a dandified emigrant who never could reconcile himself to summer weather at Christmas, and the trick the sun has of making an exposure of himself on the wrong side of the earth "It is what I've not been used to, don't you know."

Of course there were many and very serious drawbacks unavoidable in a new country. Cattle and sheep unaccustomed to the rank grass died by hundreds. Many perished in the winter veldt fires, before the people had gathered experience, and knew the ways of the land. In a few months scores of men of substance were reduced to poverty.

The spot selected for their first settlement is about three miles north of the town, Here they rested, each man building his house (" voor-eerst ") near to where he had spanned out his wagon. There was certainly an attempt at streets, but they were neither straight nor regular, nor parallel. The houses looked as if they had fallen by accident, like potatoes out of a basket. In the centre was erected, after the settlement of the community, a long narrow building, about 8 feet high, with walls of sod, and roof of thatch, unglazed openings for windows, and a door which was more frequently broken than whole. This served the tripple purpose of a citadel, a place of assembly, and a day-school house. I might with truthfulness add also a kraal for the town goats.

Here the people met for worship, conducted by

lay officers of the church, from 1862 to 1869. Around this building was thrown up a very strong fort, constructed of sods, having corner bastions and loop-holed all round. At one corner was an underground powder magazine, over which a guard was mounted, whose duty was to keep watch and ward throughout his waking hours. This was the "fort" or "laager." It was the wonder and admiration of the Kaffirs. It would be difficult to estimate the pacific effect it had on the surrounding tribes. It inspired a wholesome respect, especially the loop-holes, and the powder magazine. It was really a very creditable structure for purposes of defence. There was nothing to equal it from King William's Town to Petermaritzburg.

For two years or more the Griquas lived together around the laager, making frequent excursions through the country, each selecting his farm and doing something in the way of ploughing, planting and building in preparation for occupying it. The farms nearest the laager were taken up, and worked almost at once—such as the farms now occupied by Scott, Turton, Bowles, Salzer, etc. As the sense of security increased, the people spread out. Each Burgher was to have a farm of 3000 acres as nearly as could be guessed ("groot omtrent"), for which he had to pay 10/- for the title-deed if he choose to take it out, and £2 annual quit rent. These sums might be paid *in kind* so long as there was difficulty in getting produce exchanged for cash. The Burgher had also to provide and keep in readiness horse, saddle, bridle, and powder horn, and he himself was expected promptly to respond to the call of the Field-cornet of his Ward for military duty, and that at any hour day or night.

The conditions of settlement were as follows:—

Memorandum of the Conditions on which His Excellency the High Commissioner thinks it expedient that the Griquas should occupy a certain tract of country lying between British Kaffraria and Natal, and under which conditions, if the Griquas are determined to abandon their present territory, the High Commissioner will raise no objection to their occupying the country alluded to.

A tract of unoccupied country lying on the south-east side of Drakensberg Mountains, between the sources of the Umzimvooboo and the Umzimkooloo Rivers, to be defined after consultation with Adam Kok, by a Commissioner appointed by the High Commissioner, which country the Griquas shall occupy as British subjects.

Captain Adam Kok to receive a commission as Justice of the Peace for such territory, and for the present to administer justice among his own people, under the laws, rules and regulations now enforced in Griqualand.

It being intended by this arrangement that whilst all the powers Captain Adam Kok possesses for controlling his people and punishing offenders should be maintained, he should, in addition thereto, receive all powers which a Justice of the Peace possesses within the Colony of the Cape of Good Hope.

The Griquas to subdivide amongst themselves the lands they are thus to occupy.

Surveys are to be made of the several farms assigned to the Griquas, as soon as the proprietor of such farms may find it convenient to pay for the cost of survey.

The High Commissioner is to guarantee possession of each such farm to its occupant against all British subjects as fully and securely as if it were held under grant from the Crown, and to issue titles to this effect as soon as the surveys have been completed.

Quitrents to be paid on the same principles as in British Kaffraria, say about £5 per annum for an ordinary farm in the country to be occupied by the Griquas.

The same fees for licenses, &c. to be paid as in the Colony of the Cape of Good Hope.

All sums thus raised within the territory occupied by the Griquas to be expended exclusively in defraying the expenses of administration or in the improvement of that tract of country.

Colonial Office, 1st August, 1860.

These conditions are said to have been hurriedly prepared by Sir George Grey on the eve of his recall.

The new Governor, Sir Philip Woodhouse, seems to have taken little or no notice of the Conditions of the Griqua settlement. "Out of sight out of mind." Shortly after the Trek, war between the Boers and the Basutos broke out, and probably this diverted attention from Griqua affairs. At any rate, the promised officer did not come. When Kok reminded the Governor of the arrangement, he was told to manage as best he could, he would not be interfered with. This was repeated to the Chief and some of his Councillors in Cape Town in 1868 when they went down to confer and purchase canon, ammunition, etc. The following are Adam Kok's statements on this subject: "When I went to Cape Town (1868), I found Sir Philip Woodhouse opposed to accepting any responsibility respecting me. Sir Philip told me distinctly that I must look entirely to my own resources for my protection, etc., and, that, in effect, I was entirely independent of the Government." Thus, again, Kok and his Raad were left to organise their government practically as a sovereign state, and, in fact, did so. They made treaties. (Treaty making has always been a Griqua hobby, a kind of august-royal pastime.)

GRIQUA LAAGER (FORT) and CHURCH, 1869.

REV. W. DOWER.

No.
No.
GOUVERNEMENT VAN NIEUW GRIQUALAND
PRO REGE LEGE ET GREGE
EEN POND STERLING
1
EEN POND STERLING
1
VOLGENS BESLUIT VAN DEN HOOG-ED. VOLKSRAAD
van den 5den November, 1867.
WAARBIJ DIT GOUVERNEMENTSPAPIER TOT EEN BEDRAG VAN
TIEN DUIZEND PONDEN STERLING
wordt uitgegeven onder verband van alle Onroerende Gouvernements Eigendommen
HEEFT HETZELVE EENE GEDWONGENE KOERS VOOR
TIEN JAREN,
VAN AF DEN 1sten JANUARY, 1868
en zal na verloop van dien tyd jaarlyks tot een bedrag
VAN VYF DUIZEND PONDEN STERLING WORDEN VERNIETIGD.
Mount Currie

They negotiated exchange of territory with Natal and rectification of boundaries. They decided to issue paper money, actually had it printed, but never issued it. They waged war. They tried and convicted criminals, and executed men found guilty of murder. They elected a Volksraad, and held half-yearly Parliaments.

Let us look at the constitution of this unique little native state.

The chief officer was elected, and took as his style or title "KAPTYN." Later on we shall see what manner of man he was. The Privy or Executive COUNCIL was almost entirely composed of full-blooded Griquas. Charles Brisley, a young Englishman, was Secretary, and gradually acquired influence and power. He learned to speak and write Dutch—the official language—fairly well. In the Raad there was one man of slave extraction, *Titus Klein*, whose name will come up later on in another connection.

The VOLKSRAAD consisted of about a dozen elected representatives, two out of each Ward. They were supposed to have the control of the finances—*when there were any*. The available assets were four-footed—sheep, goats, cattle, horses. They had a singular knack of straying away, and never in any case straying back again. The cash-box was the pasturage of the Treasurer's farm or the area of the Government kraal. The banker was a Kaffir herd boy. The decisions of the Volksraad were sent up to the Privy Council, and were often discussed in a free-and-easy style on the stoep of the Chief's house, while the Councillors were drinking coffee amid clouds of tobacco smoke. The Volksraad nominally and constitutionally granted farms and erven, but, as a matter of fact, farms were often granted without its knowledge or consent, even sometimes contrary to its wishes. The appearance of political power satisfied the ambitions of the Commons, except in the cases of a few fiery spirits among them. The *Volksraad* gave the opportunity for talk; and talk soothed all grievances and healed nearly all wounds. Kok's policy was to retain the real power in his own hands and he manœuvred so as to give his policy practical effect. To this task he brought all his exceptional tact, ingenuity and resourcefulness. Occasionally there were storms in the tea-pot, a political crisis, but never a change of Ministry.

The *Volksraad* was a wonderful anachronism Its sittings were held half-yearly, and lasted as long as the commissariat held out. It was very free-and-easy both as to its composition and conduct of business. Very little real business was done, and very imperfect accounts of its proceedings kept. After a session was over, it was no uncommon occurrence for discussion to arise as to what had been decided. Often no one knew, but all knew "*de praat wat was gepraat door de mensche die het de praat gepraat*" "the talk which was talked by the people who talked the talk," that sufficed. The Deputies were hospitably entertained at Government expense during the session. Its length depended on the size of the animal slaughtered. When the beef gave out the House rose. No beef, no business, was the unwritten, but standing rule of this Assembly. It was a simpler and more effective extinguisher to Parliamentary oratory than our modern closure The cooking operations for these "*Achtbare Heeren*" were carried on close to the House of Parliament, and the big pot was so placed that members while in session could both see the progress of the operations and inhale grateful odours, as an earnest of the coming feast.

Old *Piet Draai* made frequent visits to the kitchen to light his pipe. He was admitted to be the best judge of the earliest moment when the beef was eatable. When Piet's voice was heard proclaiming the joyful news "Kerls de kos is gaar," "Gentlemen the beef is cooked," the house rose with a stampede. These Griqua Parliamentary dinners were held much after the primitive fashion which obtained in England in the days of good King Alfred. The simplicity of manners saved the little State manifold needless costs in the way of crockery, cutlery, and napery. The form of Government was roughly on the lines of the British constitution. Imitation of the white man was the unacknowledged, although the real rule of procedure. "*De Engelsche maken zoo,*" "The English act so." Beyond that there was no appeal.

It will be interesting to glance at a few specimen subjects of discussion.

Coos Magerman has not paid his quit-rent for some years. He says he has no money, no stock, no grain The member for Mt Currie remarks: "You can't take blood out of a stone." The member for Under Zuurberg declares that the Government must be supported. Another is indignant and tells how Coos' daughter was married the previous week, that her bridal array must have cost several years' quit-rent, besides the ox that was slaughtered, and the oceans of coffee consumed during the week's festivities. Resolved to make inquiry and consider the case next session. Things look a bit rough for "Coos."

Hans Beyers claims half the Ingeli forest. The Field-cornet made a mistake in describing the boundaries of Han's farm. It was found that the Field-cornet himself could not write nor yet read. His son Karel wrote for his father, the certificate under which he holds the farm, but there is some difficulty in reading it, and more in understanding it. Resolved to appoint a Commission to examine and report next month.

Stafford's Account against the Government is presented with an urgent request for settlement. Piet remarks that "Stafford is English, what is the hurry?" "The English make the money, why can't he wait?" "Cobus reminds the Raad that he has waited already a good year." Abraham remarks that is nothing. "Mensche die Engelsche"! "Oh these English!"

Quit-Rent Collection. Dissatisfaction is expressed at the appointment of indigent Griquas supposed to have a tendency to kleptomania to collect the quit-rent, and at the singular disappearance of stock from the Government herd before it reaches the Treasurer. No one can get the collection books to balance. "*Codig niet waar?*" "Strange is it not?" Peculation is somewhere, but echo continues to answer "Where?"

Appointment of Magistrate. The point is raised "why are Griquas only, to the exclusion of Bastards, Apprentices, Colonists, appointed to act as Magistrates?" The point is a delicate, even dangerous one, and there is silence and surprise at the temerity of the member who raises it. "*Stil kerels de kos is gaar.*" "Silence gentlemen the beef is cooked" House rises.

SOLILOQUY AND LAMENT

of a Member of the old Griqua Volksraad.

We ate the beef and scraped the bones
All round the pot propped up with stones;
We roasted mealies and ate offhand
Ere we made a law for Lilliputland.

Coffee we had and sugar galore.
"Whence?" Why man out of the Government store,
'Twas fast then feast to slackening of band,
While making laws for Lilliputland.

A law was made, a farm was given
While you winked an eye or counted seven;
For the land was ours you must understand,
And we were the Commons of Lilliputland.

We Senators chew and smoke and snuff,
When the "zaak is groot" or the beef is tough:
All round the fire we gravely stand,
To legislate for Lilliputland.

Oh, be ye British, or be ye Boer,
Mind your manners in our Kantoor;
Never attempt to play the grand,
For a Volksraad sits in Lilliputland.

Oh! the hall is empty, the fires are out,
The beef is eaten the farms sold out;
White man is "baas"—I'm off to the Rand,
'Tis Ichabod now in Lilliputland.

CHAPTER VI.

The ordinary administration of justice was committed to a Griqua Resident Magistrate, who held his appointment, not because of his knowledge of law, but as a matter of charity. The spheres of influence for Privy Council, Volksraad, and Resident Magistrate were clearly enough defined on paper, but the limitations and restrictions were often disregarded, so that there was a constant overlapping of authority. The Magistrate's decisions were more according to his ideas of justice and equity than according to statute law. He paid himself and his officials from fees of Court and fines, and gave account to nobody The restraint of an officer of Control would have been an intolerable nuisance. The Magistrate held office for a year or two, and then gave place to some other needy Griqua who had patiently waited his turn, thus to replenish his depleted exchequer. Ah me! It is still true that "some are born great, some achieve greatness, while some have greatness thrust upon them."

There is, or there was until recently (1901), to be seen any day on the streets of Kokstad a debauched and dilapidated looking man, a well known character in the town, *Klaas van der Westhuizen.* He was Magistrate late in the sixties. Thereafter he was Field-cornet in Mount Currie District for sometime after the "annexation." During Van der Westhuizen's term of office, the late Sir Harry Escombe, who as Premier of Natal represented that Colony at the Queen's Jubilee, being on one occasion on a hunting expedition, crossed from Natal into Kok's territory, and made himself guilty of some technical offence against Griqua law or usage. Van der Westhuizen had been arrested, and brought before him for trial. Escombe, who was perhaps somewhat deficient in the reverential spirit which gives honour to whom honour is due, was certainly not overawed in the presence of his worship, whose bench was a packing case set up in a mud hut. Struck with his somewhat bony appearance, he asked "if he was to be tried by that ugly chimpanzee?" *Wenzel Hemroe* was reluctantly compelled under threats to interpret these strange and daring words. Klaas, white with rage, if one could conceive of such an effect, fined the prisoner £5 for contempt of Court with the alternative of imprisonment. Needless to say the fine was paid, and the Magistrate was a rich man that day. The whole scene which I have heard described in the taal, must have been grotesque in the extreme. This was regarded as a red letter day in the annals of the Court, and henceforth Klaas was a hero. The event was often referred to with merriment and jest, and in glorification of the "slimness" of the "natie," and as one illustrious occasion when the white man had to sing small, and the man of colour was "cock of the walk."

Adam Kok did not scruple to let white men, even white men of distinction sometimes, wait his convenience. It added to his importance and dignity, though it did not sweeten the tempers or improve the language of those who waited. I remember one striking case. Late in 1870, Commissioners from the President of the Orange Free State came to the laager to see the Chief on business. They had come seeking for such testimony as would strengthen their disputed claim to the newly discovered diamond fields. Kok kept them waiting and chafing under the indignity for days before he would see them. He had not forgotten the old feuds and the secret treaty. When he did give them audience, they got little satisfaction. He was surly and grumpy. He knew that this time he had the right end of the whip. They tried hard to draw the old man, but failed, and went back with little satisfaction from their long wintry journey.

Nearly all business was carried on by barter. Of money there was very little in circulation. Wool, sheep, cattle, horses, goats, skins, timber eggs, grain, fowls, were exchanged for clothing and groceries. Under the Ingeli it was a common sight to see a man laboriously carrying wagon timber or yellow-wood planks to the stores, in order to exchange for some article required for the household.

Prices ranged about the following in 1870: horses from £2 10s to £.6, cows from £2 to £4, sheep about 10/-, goats 3/- to 5/-, trek oxen £3 to £5, wheat 12/ per muid of 200lbs, mealies 6d to 1/- a bucket, eggs 6d to 8d, fowls 3d to 6d each, sawn timber £4 for a load.

These quotations represent approximately the estimated money value of stock and produce, but it must be remembered that payment for these was made in groceries, clothing, etc These articles were sold at about three times the present rate. Traders' profits were exceptionally high, but their risks were great, and licences excessive. Besides, they were liable for war tax, and their "takings" might be decimated by disease before the four-footed assets could be brought to Natal, and converted into coin of the realm or its equivalent. Mr. T O. Hall about 1872 had £500 value of his takings feeding and fattening near the Umtamfuna in Natal. Lung-sickness came and reduced them to about £100 value

When the "Trek" began the Griquas had the Rev. W. B. Philip as their minister. He was a man of gentle and amiable disposition, held deservedly in high affection and esteem by the body of the people. He was unsparing in his denunciations of wrongdoing without respect of persons. His fidelity brought on him the displeasure of the powers that be

The Church, Parsonage and School at Philipolis were sold for something like £3000, while other landed property belonging to the church was sold for £4000. Of these sums, only about £500 was paid in cash and deposited in the bank at Colesberg. The purchase price was secured by mortgage bonds on valuable property to be paid off after a given time when the people had reached their new home. Meantime the interest would be available for the minister's support. He was to accompany them, and after a visit to Cape Town joined them at Hanglip in the south of Basutoland. During Mr Philips absence, the Bond holders, in a way not to their credit, got the Finance Committee of the Church persuaded to consent to a transference of the bonds from valuable to valueless property. On Mr Philip's return he denounced the dishonesty of the transaction on both sides, and pointed out the almost certain loss to the Church in certain contingencies. The result was rupture between the minister and the chiefs and the men who had been principal actors in the transaction, ending in Mr Philip's resignation and retirement, to take up the work, he did so long and so well, in the rising town of Queenstown. Thus all the carefully laid plans for the erection of new buildings, for church and school work, in the new country went to the wall. There was bungling and knavery in the whole transaction. Now they had no minister, and could not have supported one if they had had him They had no buildings and no money to erect them. Just then the Free State-Basuto war broke out. All the Civil Courts of the Orange Free State were closed for years in consequence, and when civil business was resumed, the agents had so manipulated matters that (culpably or not, it is difficult, perhaps impossible, to say) all that remained of the splendid provision made for Church work was the £500 in the Colesberg Bank and £1340 recovered in 1874, after much litigation.

And so it came about that for seven years the Griqua Church was without a settled pastor, and that in the crisis of its history, when, most of all, he was needed. During those years the church officers kept up the services without a break. The late *Rev Mr Jenkins*, and also *Rev. Mr. Eva*, Wesleyan missionaries at Emfundesweni, Pondoland, occasionally visited them and administered sacraments. One "*Cobus Constabel*," still alive (1900) was appointed *Marriage Officer*. Those church officers did not fail to maintain discipline. It is to their credit that when the chief himself became guilty of conduct unworthy of a Christian professor, they disciplined him even to exclusion from church privileges. He never became repentent, at least, he never sought restoration to church fellowship, though he attended Divine Service with exemplary regularity, and helped in all the external affairs of the church.

Despairing of getting a European minister, they elected to the pastorate a very worthy and respected deacon, *Hans or Johannes Bezuidenhout*. He was duly ordained, in 1869, by the late Revs R. Taylor, of Cradock, and James Read, of Philipton. He was a good man, upright, honest, sincere His education was very elementary, but he knew his Bible well, and had a large experience of church work. Poor Hans was placed in a false position from the first. He was required to leave his farming, and the church undertook to pay him £150 per annum in cash. The most extraordinary part of it is that there was not that amount of coin in the country at the time. The congregation failed to fulfil its promise. In a very short time the good man had to return to his farm or starve. He remained nominally pastor till 1877, preaching occasionally. A day school had been conducted up to 1870 by a blind man, *William Trowbridge*, assisted by his nephew. The £50 per annum payable to the Griquas, under the provisons of one of the treaties, for the payment of a teacher, was continued, although the treaty was considered to have lapsed.

Such, briefly, was the political and ecclesiastical position of the tribe when, at the request of the London Missionary Society, and not a few of my ministerial brethren in the Colony, I paid a visit to *Nomansland* in 1869. Grass fires, change of pasturage, winter colds, had decimated their stock, and reduced nearly all the Griquas to comparative poverty. A few were still fairly well off. These could still drive to church or Raad in the family spring wagon with prancing horses or excellent mules. They still ate the meat and drank the milk of their own flocks. The earth brought forth plentifully, if only kindly entreated. Wheat was abundant; various fruits, such as apples, pears, peaches, nectarines, quinces, grew luxuriously, equal in quality to any produced in South Africa. Mealies, pumpkins, and all European vegetables grew with the minimum of labour. Water was abundant, fountains, spruits, rivers, everywhere. Yet many of the people were wretchedly poor. How they subsisted was a mystery. The problem is, I understand, still unsolved. With a few exceptions the Griquas are not fond of work. That is putting it very mildly indeed. The fact is they hate work—look upon it as a sore necessity, tinged with degradation. Can we altogether blame them? This aversion to work is in their marrow and their bones. They drank it in with their mother's milk. Their ancestors never worked They hunted, they milked the cows, and later on, they sheared the sheep, and drove the spare cattle to market or to the trader's wagon to sell. Since the days when the emigrant Boers crossed the Orange River, and in their attitude to labour, the Griquas have taken them as the products of Christian civilisation. To use a vulgarism, they take their cue from them. The Boers were "*Christe mensche*," and theirs was the only type of Christian civilisation with which these people were familiar. Is the ordinary Boer passionately fond of work? Nay, verily! He can and does make other men work, but he will beat all comers in the ingenuity he brings to bear on the problem, how to get hard and coarse work done without doing it himself. The Boer thinks, if he does not say, "Why should a man do hard and coarse work if he can employ another man to do it for him?" But the Griquas went a step further, and said, "Why do it at all, if you can avoid doing it?" He solved the problem of living by means of the products of the chase and the milk of his cows. "Why," he said, "toil and sweat when you can eat venison and drink milk and sleep half the day in the sun?" "*Alla mensche ik is nie gek ne.*" (Why! I am not a fool). The time of trial came when the game was all gone and the cows were all dead. That test came to the Griquas in *Nomansland*, and as a people they went down under it

Civilisation creates new wants. The supply of these wants soon drains the natural resources dry, unless industry and skill produce increase of capital to meet the additional outlay. Without this increase of industry, civilisation puts the beggars' staff into the hands of the civilised, and civilises them off the face of the earth. If a heathen tribe accepts Christianity, and in its train the most rudimentary civilisation, the Gospel which saves the soul must become an inspiration to work or the tribe is doomed. These elementary principles of political economy, these teachings of Christianity itself, have been persistently preached to these people. They have listened with deaf ears, and to-day they are landless, almost homeless waifs, servants, or *bywooners*. The average Griqua, if he could not plough a large piece of land, would not condescend to dig a small piece If he could not have a wagon, he would not condescend to use a Scotch cart. A handbarrow was his abhorrence. The spade, the cart, the barrow, meant that the actual stress and strain must fall on his own shoulders, and he would have none of it.

CHAPTER VII.

At this time (1869) there were very few Europeans in the country *Charles Brisley* was Government Secretary, *Edward Barker* was managing Brisley's farm at "*Elands Kop*;" *T. O. Hall* was trading, and of whom more hereafter; *Bowden*, who managed Stafford's store; *Saunders*, formerly Astistant Traffic Manager on one of the great railways of England, was doing carpenter work; *Erridge*, a very competent accountant, was farming; the brothers *Donald* and *Thomas Strachan* were farming and transport riding at Clydesdale;

Archie Scott, a Scotch blacksmith, was farming near Reit Vley; *Van Wyhe*, an Amsterdamer, was farming at Sneezewood, rapidly accumulating wealth by cattle-rearing, growing mealies and wool, making butter and cheese, braying riems, and tanning leather, making veldschoens and rough saddlery; *Mr Hully* was farming on the banks of the Umizmukulu, and also doing the work of an Evangelist among the Kaffirs, in connection with the Wesleyan Methodist Church. His work formed the nucleus of the Station at Entembeni. These, I think, constituted the entire white population in 1869. Only three survive—D. Strachan, Hall, and Scott.

The Missionary Society which deputed me to visit the Griquas left me free to settle among them, or to take up work elsewhere. I reached *Mount Currie* Laager about the middle of August, and was lodged with the *Rev William Murray*, who was then conducting a boarding school for the benefit of several more advanced Griqua lads. I preached in the long, low, dark building inside the fort or laager. Through the open holes left for light in the side walls a cold wintry wind blew. The few very rough seats and the "rust-banken," and camp stools brought from the houses were occupied by the men; the women sat on the floor, back against the wall, legs drawn up, and the whole body closely covered with a kaross, so that only a mass of hair was seen with the two eyes looking through the opening. They had a very fierce appearance. My pulpit was a biggish packing box, set on end, top and back removed, and a sloping board fixed. The attendance was fairly good, and the singing very creditable indeed, though, of course, there was no instrumental accompaniment. On the evening of this, my first Sunday among the Griquas, it began to snow, and snowed heavily all night and next day. By Tuesday morning the snow lay 18 inches deep. The Griquas were practically snowed up, and most of them in bed. We should have perished from cold and hunger, but for a box of provisions which, happily, I had brought with me. For fuel, we used up certain timbers of the roof which we considered could be spared, and put to a merciful use. The storm lives in the memories of the older Griquas as "*De Groote Kopok*," and the season of it was a time to date from "*De jaar van de groote Kopok*," just as in Scotland, fifty years ago, people spoke of "the year o' the muckle storm." The burning timber heated the chimney, melted the snow around it, and the cold sleet came dropping down into our necks, if we sat near enough to get any heat. The fire proving a failure, Mr Murray and I took to tripping the light fantastic toe in the big empty shop, forming part of the house, before betaking ourselves to the sparse supply of blankets. Not a single person looked near us.

It had been arranged that I should go early in the week to

Reit Vley, for the double purpose of celebrating a wedding, and having an opportunity of seeing that part of the country. We started before the snow had melted, and experienced not a little difficulty in ploughing our way through the deep snow-drifts on the Zuurberg. It may interest present residents to know that the main road to Natal, via *Reit Vley*, in those days passed along the face of Mount Currie, till it joined the present road on the neck north-east from the town, then past the back of Gunther's dwelling-house, through the river at the bottom of his lands, over the flats past Salzer's, and up the face of the mountain joining the more recent Natal road on the top of the hill.

During my three weeks' stay in *Nomansland* I saw a good deal of the country, and learned all I could of the condition cf church and people. At the end of my visit the question was raised, "Would I decide to remain among them?" I consented on certain conditions, one of which was that they should decide to leave the Laager and build a new township on the present site of Kokstad. This was a *sine qua non*. Other sites had been mentioned, and had their advocates and their merits too. My vote, or rather my condition, came when the scales were nearly evenly balanced My conditions were accepted at a very large and enthusiastic meeting, and I undertook to return and settle with my family among them as soon as possible. Before leaving I examined the proposed plan of the township, which was the work of *Edward Barker*, and approved of all the arrangement of streets, etc. About the last days of my stay Mr Murray and I had a good look at the site and the water supply. By means of a spirit-level fixed to a moveable beam, mounted on a rude tripod, a kind of extemporised Theodolite, we satisfied ourselves as to the facility of irrigation, and roughly marked the course of the proposed water furrow. At the request of the old chief we planted a stick firmly into an antheap, on the spot where we thought the centre of the town should be, *From that as a starting place the subsequent survey was carried out*. On the top of the stick I fixed a white pocket handkerchief. When we had finished our work we sat around that antheap, boiled our coffee kettle, discussed our homely lunch, and enjoyed the delightful prospect around us. There, three miles off, was the grand old mountain putting on its spring dress, the young grass, with its delicate green shoots, intermingling with the brown grass of last year. The hoary, rugged crest towering aloft 7297 feet above sea-level seemed so near in the clear atmosphere that one felt as if you could reach forth your hands and touch it. "Double the height of Table Mountain, to which in form and play of cloud it bears some resembrance, it is only half the height from its own base, and is yet more unlike in being green to the foot of its rocky headpiece. As a lair of the tropical thundercloud, whence issue lightnings and voices and thunderings and an earthquake, and great hail. its superiority admits of no question. A kaleidoscope ever-varying, and never repeating the same view, it will change its aspect five times in as many minutes. One half is sometimes hidden by a cloud, stretching up to the general cloud-level, and in a minute the other half will seem to have no existence; then the head peeps out of a drapery massed in folds about the base, or the base appears and the head is cut of, or the whole is enveloped in fleecy cloud." Away in the east lay the Zuurberg range, and the fertile valley of the *Umzimslava;* to the west the ranges around *Nungi Nek* and the *Umzimvubu Poort;* south lay the majestic *Ingeli* chain, in whose bowels are believed to be stores of mineral wealth, and over whose crest lay the Colony of Natal. I know of no township in South Africa which presents to the beholder a grander panorama of the everlasting hills, or a more extensive, uninterrupted prospect.

It has been said, by them of old, that young men shall see visions, and old men shall dream dreams. We two were on the dividing line, and shared the fortunes and privileges of both old and young. We saw some visions and dreamed some dreams on that eventful day. The nearest house, or hut, or home was a good mile away, under what is now the barrack kopje. The virgin soil on which we stood had never tasted spade, or felt the tear of the ploughshare. There was nothing on all the ridge to be seen but the brown winter grass, knee deep, and hundreds of antheaps, big and little. By faith and by fancy we looked into the future and saw other things. We saw broad streets with shady trees and running water, stately churches, thronged with worshippers; "playful children just let loose from school"; shops and offices and halls, parks and gardens, hospitals and prisons, roads and bridges. Then imagination took a higher flight, and from its lofty point of vision it saw a long burnished double thread winding out and in among the hills, and on it came, puffing along the iron horse of commerce, bringing the merchandise of many climes, and settlers to fill up the waste places of this land of promise, and to make the bare ridge one of the fairest cities of this Southern land. These dreams and visions are, year by year, being realised, in fact. The handsome Town Hall, opened at the beginning of 1901, and the serious proposals to pipe the town water and utilise the driving power of the *Umzimslvaa* to light the town by electricity, remind one of the adage, "The dreamer dreamed fond dreams, and dreaming dreamed them true."

My lyre is somewhat cracked and cranky, but I cannot resist the temptation to thrum her strings a bit, in celebration, of this never-to be-forgotten day.

Middle of Market Square, September, 1869.

Now waves yon white flag o'er the virgin soil,
A point for measure and a call to toil.
Draw long the furrow, coax yon crystal stream.
Here flowed its wat rs in my last night's dream.

High on Mount Currie's brown and barren crest,
There fell a gleam of glory from the west;
The old hill smiled, as if it fain would speak,
And greetings seemed to pass from peak to peak.

Methought I heard upon the evening breeze,
Borne from the cliffs three miles across the leas,
A hum that sounded strangely like Ha! Ha!
But soon it burst into a loud "Hurrah"!

What could it be? Like this to me it seems,
Mount Currie's bowels with living water teams;
Her great internal caverns fill and flow
To useless waste upon the plains below.

'Tis not for this she filters with such pains
Dew, mist, and rain through countless fissured veins;
The broad plain at her feet proclaims her plan,
Her generous stores are chiefly meant for man.

She smiles at last to spy the founder's pin
Mark off the spot, whence work should now begin;
The fluttering flag was pledge that now, at last
The weary years of watery waste were past.

Like mother's arms the flanking hills stretch wide,
To tell the wanderer here he may abide.
Those hoary peaks that ever pierce the sky
Are God's stone fingers, pointing men on high.

* * * *

Thirty Years Thereafter.

Without a break for ten years three times told
Not less thro' summer heat or winter cold,
Still, bubbling water from that fountain springs,
And priceless blessing to the people brings.

Where antheaps thickly strewed the silent plain,
Where long grass waved with every summer rain,
Now stands to-day, a city, built foursquare,
With hall of justice, and the house of prayer.

The farmers meet upon the Market place.
The skilful lawyer pleads to gain his case.
The merchant spreads to view his tempting wares,
And parsons tie the knots for happy pairs.

Church bells salute the opening Sabbath morn.
Loud, oft, and shrill sounds out the postman's horn.
The schoolboy shouts to see the bounding ball.
The soldier answers to the bugle call.

May every good attend the growing town,
The mountain's smiling face forget to frown·
Its people working all with head and hand.
It might become the glory of the land.

I returned to my home in the village of *Uniondale*, via Natal, and came back to Mount Currie with my wife and children, reaching the end of our journey on the 19th of May, 1870, after spending three months in a wagon. From the *Gatberg* Settlement, now Maclear, there was only the roughest track. Frequently the wagon had to be kept on its wheels by all hands holding on to the riems fastened to the tent. Drifts were the most serious difficulties. From Gatberg we saw no human habitation until we reached the vicinity of Matatiela, Our way for many miles lay through the ashes of the burnt-off veldt

At Matatiela the Basuto chief Makwai had his kraal on the top of the mountain. Here, too, was an Irishman, O'Reily, Adam Kok's magistrate for the district, who lived in a sorely dilapidated hut on the hill. We were outspanned on the spot where the village now stands, close beside a tree, the only one on the flat. Beneath that tree I had preached to *Makwai's* Basutos on the previous year, and here I preached to them again. This tree remained a *well-known landmark* for years thereafter. I saw it last in 1880, a few days before the outbreak of the Basutos.

O'Reilly sent a message to say that if we could supply him with a piece of soap he would be able to do himself the pleasure of paying us a visit. This representative of law and authority was duly provided with this facility for much-needed ablution, and having made himself presentable, came down from his exalted station to offer us a welcome.

> "Hard was his lot and lodgings you'll allow,
> A wigwam that would hardly serve a sow ;
> His garment was a topcoat and an old one,
> His meal a mealie and a cold one."

The last stage of the journey to *Mount Currie* had to be performed fasting. Ay! verily, fasting, for we could purchase nothing to eat, and our stock of provisions was exhausted. No bread, no meal, no milk, no coffee, tea, sugar, or salt. The road in those days lay along the top of the range of hills, back of *Klopper's* farm, past "*Elands Kop*," past *Villander Gou's*, through the "*Droevig*," between "*Nairn*" and "*Fair View*" (new names), then over the neck and into *Mount Currie Laager*, past the intake of the Kokstad water supply.

At the "*Laager*" we were accommodated in the best house in the place—which was not saying much—a disused shop, the same building which Mr Murray had occupied on the previous year, and the scene of our sufferings. *Mr Murray* had left *Mount Currie*, and gone to live near Mount Fletcher, to work among the people of *Lehanna*. Here, for the present, we settled down. Mrs. Barker, then *Miss Edward*, my wife's sister, had come with us, at the invitation of the Griquas, to conduct the day school, and she immediately commenced in the house inside the Fort. She continued to conduct the school till July, 1879, when Mr Murray took her place.

CHAPTER VIII.

During the interval of my absence, September till May, the new township had been laid out, working from the flagstaff planted by Mr Murray and myself in September The survey and ploughing out of the lines of streets had been done by the late *Edward Barker*, but as yet no house of any kind stood on the site. During the interval mentioned, the Griquas had also "taken out" the water furrow, not, certainly, in a very effective fashion, but sufficiently well to secure an abundant supply. Since then, there has been no change to speak of made on that furrow, except widening and deepening. The furrow was constructed by free labour. Each Veldt-Kornet, in turn, called out the able-bodied men of his ward for a week or so. Government supplied food, or, at least, beef, coffee, sugar, and tobacco, and the thing was done. The cost of introducing a water supply is usually a first charge on the finances of a new town. KOKSTAD has had its splendid water supply, from the first, free of any great municipal outlay. On this ground the Griquas have set up a claim for special privileges, and certainly the fact should beget, at least, kindly consideration On the other hand, the Griquas conveniently forget that, elsewhere, people buy and do not "take" their erven, and the purchase money goes towards initial costs, such as water supply.

Within a month after outspanning at the Laager, I had begun housebuilding on the new site, or, rather, begun brick-making. The whole establishment, Church, School, and Parsonage I had planned, and laid down on paper before a sod was cut. To that plan I, approximately, adhered till the whole was completed some twelve years thereafter.

An Englishman, Morris, took the contract, an arrangement which proved a huge failure. This same Morris was blown to pieces in the explosion of 1878.

The chief and his Councilors urged that the Parsonage must be large enough, not only to accommodate an ordinary family, but to serve as a kind of *Royal Hotel*, in which Colonial political agents might be housed during their visits on business. Up to the Chief's death, and, indeed, for some time thereafter, until a hotel was opened in the town, the claims on our lodging capacity and hospitality quite justified these proposals.

My time was now fully occupied, preaching, visiting, exploring the country, and superintending the erection of my dwelling-house. The duty of attending to the ailments of the sick was forced on me by the isolation of our position, for the nearest medical man was 65 miles distant. My wife was more successful than I was in the treatment of the sick. But, in the dispensing of medicine we must, between us, have done some good and useful work, for at the end of the second year the Griqua Government provided us with a very complete little

Dispensary, at an outlay of £90. Dental and surgical operations taxed my slender resources of experience and skill Once, while riding across the veldt, my attention was arrested by a white rag fluttering in the wind above the long grass. A European trader, over-estimating his personal capacity, for taking in Kaffir beer, had fallen from his horse and broken his leg, and lay helpless. With much trouble I had him removed to the nearest Griqua house, until lately an outhouse on the farm "*Mooimeisjesfontein*," on which *Mr. Z. Bowles* now resides. There I did the best I could with a very impatient patient. Whether he or I was to blame, was long a subject of friendly dispute, but certain it is that when he began to walk, the foot was found to be set at an obtuse angle to the direct line of progression. Good-humouredly, he admitted that he had occasionally turned and twisted the broken limb after setting, but that "a squint foot was better than no foot at all."

Our position was very isolated indeed. The nearest post office was *Umzimkulu Drift*, 50 miles away, from whence we received letters and papers once a month, if we chose to send for them. Regular post there was none. Adam Kok did not believe in sending for letters; he thought he was better without them. His theory was "if letters bring good news they can wait, and if the news happens to be bad, well, better that they don't come at all. Why, then, *send* for letters?" *Dr. Calloway*, of Spring Vale, afterwards first Bishop of the Diocese of St. John's, was the nearest doctor. He was not practising, so that really the nearest available medical help was Pietermaritzburg, 100 miles away. We saw Europeans very seldom, excepting the very few around us. Indeed, there were only four in the Laager besides ourselves. These were *Hall, Brisley, Bowden, Saunders*. We were, however, usually so busily occupied that we had little time to think of, or mourn over, the absence of "*Society*."

While the Parsonage was being erected, the Griquas began to realise that they had committed themselves to the "TREK" Removal was now in the air. Hitherto the discussion had gathered around the question of *Site*. Now, that was settled once for all. To trek, or not to trek, that was now the question. Some urged an immediate and simultaneous removal. Not a few declared their belief, that the projected township would come to nought The lazy lot who basked all day in the sunny side of the sod hut, now affirmed with energy and heat of feeling. "*De ezels zullen eerst hoorns hebben 'eer die plek en dorp zal worden*": "Asses will grow horns before that place will become a town." These conservative gentlemen, whose descendents have not yet died out, threw cold water on every scheme involving effort or self-sacrifice. They were "too poor to build," which, translated into honest language, meant they were too lazy. "The site was too far away from the fuel"; "the water would give out" ; "the opgaaf (or rate of 5s. per annum) was too high" ; "the Pondos would attack them when they left the protection of the Fort" ; "the new minister's building schemes were the impossible dreams of a mad roinek. Who would follow him?"

These ragged gentlemen "Burgers," all of them, ever seated in the sun, discussing Griqua politics, nursing old grievances, and hatching new ones, were like so many pin-pricks to me, until I got to know who was who. The most enterprising of the people were not at first at all enthusiastic about removing. I kept on begging of the chief to urge the people, by proclamation, to take up their town erven. Let an angel from heaven try and establish a city in the wilds with such unpromising material and he will not have his sorrow to seek. I write feelingly, for the memory of these worries comes back to me like the ghosts of buried griefs Up to the end of 1870 the only erven "*taken up*," so far as I can remember, were :—

1. The six erven given to the Griqua Church.
2. Government erf, on which the *Public Offices* now stand.
3. Adam Kok's erf, the site of the old Palace.
4. *Charles Brisley's* erf, on which Mr Dold's shop now stands.
5. The erf granted to Mrs Barker, and on which she is now living.
6. The erven between Dold's shop and the *Royal Hotel*, taken up by the members of Kok's *Council*.

The bulk of the erven were unalloted. There was a manifest unwillingness to "*take up*" erven even as there was hesitation and delay in taking up farms. Be it remembered that there were no charges, no upset price, no office fee. The best erven in town went a-begging for owners. This must appear almost incredible, yet it is absolutely true, without any exaggeration.

Here, I would venture to insert a little incident connected with the erection of the very first building on the site of the township. In September, 1869, I was in Durban, on my way home, after my first visit to *Nomansland*. I had to wait the return of the old s.s. "*Natal*," and, feeling the heat I went to a certain tailor, Mr L , well-known in the town, and asked him to make for me a thin garment. He took the measure, looked at me, with an enquiring and curious glance, and said, "Do you preach in Dutch?" To this I replied, "Yes." "Ah! good. I will send the coat home to-morrow." He did. He had fitted me out with a real Geneva clerical coat, with buttons many down the front, tassels, tags, and wrist decorations, "*an a' that.*" I paid the good man, and, packing up this wonderful garment, I brought it home, to the merriment of my friends, and next year I brought it back in my baggage to *Mount Currie*.

Rev. W. Dower & Rev. W. Murray selecting site of Kokstad.

KOKSTAD MARKET AND GOVERNMENT OFFICES, 1901.

MR. G. C. BRISLEY.

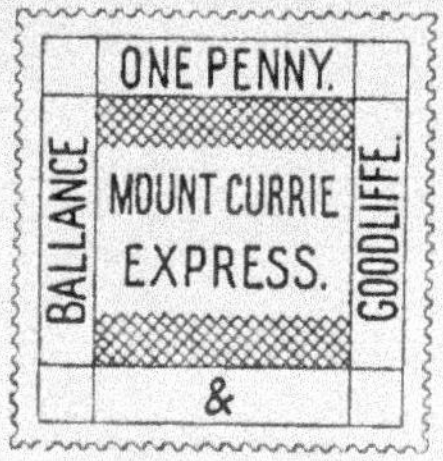

Seal of the Griqua Government.

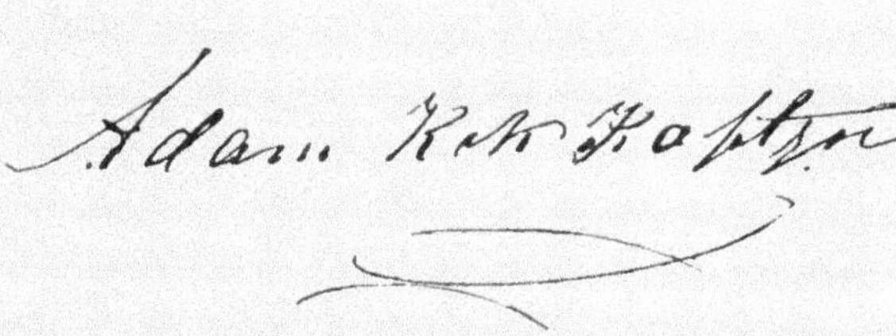

Francis Moentjes, the original grantee of the farm *Glenrock*, eagerly jumped at my offer to give him the clerical coat for the building of the sod walls of a *wagon house* He built the walls and wore the coat. Its possession made him the admiration and envy of all the young swells of the Laager. So it came to pass that the very first building erected in Kokstad was paid for by a Geneva clerical coat, made by mistake, by old Mr. L., the Durban tailor, a worthy old Christian patriarch ! The coat and the house have both gone to dust long ago. I give them both a place in the annals of the city.

Early in 1871 a great gathering was summoned by the Chief. The clans mustered in great force, and on the *Market Square*, round the antheap with the flagstaff, they presented a very creditable appearance. A good deal of political heat and ferment had been generated by the secret intriguing of *Smith Pommer*, under Zuurberg. The causes of dissatisfaction seemed to me, then, and equally now, very visionary and groundless. Sifted to their actual significance, they really amounted to jealousy, on the part of *Pommer*, of the influence which *Charles Brisley* was daily acquiring over the Chief and the Raad.

Without entering into delicate questions, as to the social position *Brisley* chose to take up, or his status in the Government, let me here say, with all candour and frankness, that he rendered valuable service to the Chief and the people. His advice on all political matters was wise and disinterested, as far as it was possible for a man, in his position, to be. His standard of ethics, his ideals of life, and mine were widely different and irreconcilable. He did not profess to be a religious man. Though, for obvious reasons, he was not specially cordial, or sympathetic to myself, yet he was frank, open, and fair. I do not think that he ever directly used his great power with the Chief to the injury of myself or of my work.

Smith Pommer meant mischief. There was a cloud on his face that day. He was as surly to speak to as a butcher's dog. I have reason to believe that he and his party intended at this "*Vergadering*" to demand and enforce *Brisley's* removal. I was assured afterwards, by credible persons, that *Pommer* and his immediate followers had weapons in readiness, and were prepared to proceed to hostilities. They were the same individuals who fought and fell with *Pommer* in the Zuurberg Kloof eight years thereafter. About midday on this historical occasion, the Chief summoned the people around his wagon. It stood almost on the spot where the Market Booth now stands He spoke pretty much as follows :—

"Burghers, we have long spoken of making a Township.
"We have sometimes not said one way about the selection of a
'*site*. That question is, happily, settled. Here is the site of

"the new town. We are gathered just about the centre of the "Market Square. Do you see the antheap and the flag-stick "there? Well, that is the centre. You see the streets are "marked off and the erven. The water is laid on, the "minister's house is nearly ready for occupation He will "move into it soon. There is the site of the Church and the "School, and here, on my right, will be the Government "Buildings. Now, I want to tell you that, according to the "decisions of the *Volksraad* and the *Uitvoerende Raad*, this is to "be our Chief Town. Every Burgher is now free to select the "erf he likes best, only see that two do not select the same erf. "Do not strive. There are plenty of erven; they are all equally "good, and of equal size. The price is nothing; only when you "have made your selection, you must register your choice with "the Secretary, who will give you a ticket of allotment. The "titles are being printed in Cape Town, and will soon be "available. The quit rent is *five shillings* a year, payable in "cash or kind. Go now and choose, and when you have all "made your selection, come back here, and I have other matters, "of public interest, to bring up for your consideration"

Adam Kok was one of the shrewdest of men. He knew the people well; he knew also human nature. Whether he was aware that *Smith Pommer* was there with hostile intent may be doubted, but he knew that something was stirring. He knew that the choosing of erven, and the registering, and the bickering would exhaust the daylight, and keep the people busy and apart. Ominous and opportune banks of cloud were shewing themselves above the horizon. The slaughtered beef was in the old Laager, not on the new township. The rain, or the darkness, or both, as well as the attractions of beef eating, would drive them to shelter in the Laager, and there would be no second meeting. By four o'clock the rain was falling heavily, and everyone was hasting away. *Kok* felt safe beside his Fort and powder magazine, and could defy *Pommer.* "*Piet*," and "*Hans*," and "*Cootje*" could bear a political grievance; in fact, without one, life would be, to them, dull as ditch water. But a summer rain, in defective clothing, without shelter, and no beef to eat, who could stand that? "*Smith goed kan maar klaar komen met zyne bedanking van Brisley, Huis toe!*" ("Smith and his supporters may manage as best they can about displacing Brisley. Let's home.") This was the first and the last time Pommer's party had the chance of action until 1878. The disaffection and intrigue continued, Riet Vley being the centre, and S. Pommer the moving spirit, until it culminated in the death of Pommer and the scattering of such of his sympathisers as survived.

CHAPTER IX.

KOKSTAD was now a Township. The erven had now registered owners, and they were negotiable property. The titles were almost immediately issued The old law prohibiting the sale of Griqua landed property to any but Burghers was still in force. Those who know the Griquas will easily believe, those who do not know them will with difficulty credit, my statement, when I say that within a few months after the issue of title, I could have bought up half the erven of the new town at from 20s. to 30s. a-piece, a muid-sackful of titles for a few pounds " *Mynheer moet toch myn erf koopen ik ben heel uit kos.* ("Buy my erf, do, please, sir, I have no food") This was the daily cry. Erven, to-day worth large sums of money, irrespective of buildings, were in my offer for ridiculous prices. An old coat, a half-worn suit of clothing would have sufficed for the purchase. I resolved that I would not buy one single erf, and kept to my resolution. I had come among the people as a missionary. It was, in my view, advisable to refrain from land-jobbing. A simple people would doubt the sincerity of the man, minister, or no minister, who would say "I advise you not to sell, but if you are resolved on selling against all advice, I am ready to buy." By and bye intending sellers came to know that the offer to sell to me, only gave me the chance to read them a hot lecture on the folly and sin they were committing against themselves and their families In many cases I might have as well spoken to the wind. The average Griqua, if he once gets the "*verkoop gedachte*," the selling fever, has neither conscience, nor reason, nor common-sense, nor ears to hear.

After many bitter disappointments, and many a weary ride between the old Laager and the new town, the Parsonage was fit for occupation. On the 19th of May, 1871, just a year after our arrival, we took up residence in the new town. Miss Edward, the teacher, remained in the Laager, alone, and occupied the house we left. We were alone in the new town. *Martinus David's* house, under the kopje, was still the nearest dwelling. I drove up to the Laager every Sunday and every Wednesday, for Divine Service. The day school was still there. Meantime, we laid the foundations of the Griqua Church. This was accomplished in the following manner. As yet we had received no part of the Church Building Fund The minister and the deacons (twelve in number), of whom, I think, only one survives, volunteered to quarry and lay down one hundred loads of building-stone on the site. At once we opened a quarry, beside a spruit on the farm "*Koppies Kraal*," right opposite the Kokstad Mill. We made a drift close by, which, thereafter, until the bridge was opened, became the entrance drift to the town, by the roads leading from the Colony and Natal. We accomplished our task, and this served as a kind of *challenge* to others to attempt something The late Lodowijk Kok was in those days a quiet, douce, prosperous farmer at *Konings Kroon*, living in the house which afterwards became the home of the Liversage family. Lodowijk volunteered to collect workers, and see the foundations of the Church put in level with the surrounding ground, *at his own costs*. He employed masons, *Apollos Bloom*, etc , and brought in his own wagon. His wife brought food and did the cooking. Lodowijk remained on the spot for a month, and completed his task. Sawyers, in the Ingeli bush, now took up the challenge, and while one felled the timber, another slipped it to the saw pit. Another did the sawing, and the last loaded it up and delivered it, *free of charge*, on the Church ground. Others began brick making. Thus a good deal of work was done by voluntary labour, until the £1340 came to hand, and from that time all work had to be paid for.

Towards the middle of 1872, two events of importance took place, each marking a further stage of progress First, *I decided to discontinue* PREACHING IN THE OLD LAAGER CHURCH, and began to conduct service in the open air, on the site of the new proposed Griqua Church The move, like every other attempt to force these people, was a distinct *failure*. I have never confessed this much to wife or child, or even allowed it to myself, until I have now put it down in writing. Yes, emphatically, a failure! It had, however, its compensations, for I learned, once for all, that I might coax, persuade, wheedle this people, but that driving was altogether out of the question. But I could not now, very well, go back on my word, and so for a time, I was in a difficulty, and feeling very small indeed. Half-a-dozen people, sitting under umbrellas with me at church, where service should be; 300 or 400, under the *holey* roof of the Laager Kerk! I felt decidedly small, beaten, thwarted. The good chief opportunely came to my assistance. I had acted with his tacit sanction, and he did not desert me. He hastily constructed a small sod house, about ten by twelve feet, close up against the north gable of the present building, and moved in there himself. This shanty was the *pro tem.* Palace.

This led to the second event—THE FORMAL REMOVAL OF THE SEAT OF GOVERNMENT *from the Laager to Kokstad.*

This took place on this wise On a certain day—unfortunately the date is lost—Kok called his Burghers up. They came in large numbers, all except those from Riet Vley and Umzimkulu, who were not invited Griquas, Kaffirs, Basutos came. He assembled them in the old Laager, and they held a sort of review, going through certain evolutions Kok dressed himself in his General's uniform—sash, belt, gold lace, epaulets, sword, etc. All this to give dignity to the occasion and weight to his words.

Without giving any explanation of his purpose he issued his orders to the Veldt Cornets, short and sharp. "Load up "the ammunition, every cartridge of it. Klaas, you see that "every article of Government property is placed on that wagon. "Span the oxen to the cannon." To the Magistrate he had issued an order to pack up all records of office, &c. "Now, trek, and all march to the "*New Town*." I had received a message from the Chief to try and be at home that day, and a hint of what was proceeding. Towards afternoon, the cavalcade, with the Chief and all his Councillors, Chief Nicholas Waterboer (Kok's son-in-law) at the head thereof, reached the town. It drew up in front of a very temporary sod house, which had been erected near to where Harvey and Greenacre's shop now stands, and all stood to attention in a half circle. The Chief, in his abrupt way, addressed me, and said, "Mr Dower will pray." The position was awkward, and somewhat embarrassing, as no official notice had been given to me of the object of the gathering. The brief devotions over, the Chief said: "From "to-day this is to be the SEAT of GOVERNMENT. Hence- "forth I myself will live here. I shall break down my house "in the old Laager. The *Volksraad* will hold its sittings here; "the *Magistrate's Court* will be held here; the *minister* will "conduct all his services here, excepting on the first Sunday "of each month. He tells me he will continue to preach in the "Laager monthly till the end of the year, but not a day longer. "The day school also will continue to be held in the Laager "only till the close of the year. The guns and ammunition will "remain here. Now, Burghers, it is time to bestir yourselves, "and build your houses, and come and make your homes here. "We are treating our minister shamefully in leaving him here "high and dry with his family, and not a soul near to him. "Think shame of yourselves!" The cannons were backed into the ammunition shed, where they remained till Captain Blyth took them over in March, 1876. Mr. Brisley then came forward and intimated that out of respect to the Kaptyn the Raads had agreed that the New Town should henceforth bear the name KOKSTAD. All this was translated into Kaffir by "*Petroos*." Then three cheers were raised for KOKSTAD, and three cheers more for the *Kaptyn*. "Huis toe."

Just about this time (middle of 1872) *Goodliffe and Balance*, of Durban, bought the old shop in the Laager for the sum of £75, exactly what the Griqua Church had given for it, four years before. With this money and the remnants of the ready cash obtained for the Philipolis property, and with the help of the people, we hurriedly ran up the Griqua Schoolroom, and, by the New Year, had it ready for church and school.

CHAPTER X.

Adam Kok now set about erecting his dwelling-house, afterwards known as "*The Palace.*" It will interest my readers to know that nearly all the carpenter work of this house was done by the late Griqua Chief *Nicholas Waterboer*, a man whose name will always figure largely in South African history. The discovery of diamonds, in what he claimed as his country, and the sudden influx of a lawless mining population, had well-nigh driven the quiet man to his wit's end. Suddenly, he found himself about the most important and sought-after individual in South Africa. Speculators and fortune-hunters buzzed round about him, day and night, like bees round a pot of sugar. He told me that for some months he could get little rest, quiet, or sleep, and life became to him not worth living. People came from all parts with all kinds of documents to sign, and all kinds of presents, not excepting cases of brandy and champagne. Many of these unscrupulous men dexterously made the most extraordinary proposals to him, as to how he could best manage to dispose of the country. They found Waterboer not the man who would readily say, "Show the inside of your purse to the outside of my hand, and there will be no more ado." They were a rollicking, jolly, sort of men, who spread the snare cunningly for his unwary feet.

> "I love a prince will bid the bottle pass,
> Exchanging with his subjects glass for glass."

Waterboer had been a strictly sober man, but from that time he acquired a taste for liquor, which ultimately proved his ruin. The conflict of claims for ownership, the self-assertiveness of the miners, the violent threats of the more determined of them, and the responsibilities of government were too much for him. He handed over his country and all his rights to the *High Commissioner*. Then came the Orange Free State authorities and the Transvaal officials, worrying his life out about beacons and boundaries, concessions and sales, treaties and promises. To his subjects he had given no formal titles; they had only prescriptive rights, and now they also came in shoals, all clamouring for some writing confirmatory of their holdings. Poor *Waterboer*, even with his £1 00 a year, was like a mouse between the teeth of a harrow. If anyone will turn to the files of the Colonial Press for '69-'70-'71, he will better understand into what a sea of trouble friend *Waterboer* was thrown. He got out of it by quietly slipping away over the mountain to *Nomans'and*.

He had a good supply of the very best carpenter's tools, and a passionate love for working in wood. Thus it came about that the chief, whose name is so prominent in the annals of South Africa, in the supreme crisis of its development, took his rest from the cares of kingship in building the house of his father in-law, and generally helping in the founding of the Town.

Very soon after taking up my residence among the Griquas, I realised that to eradicate their foolish and ridiculous notions as to the indignity of manual labour, it was necessary not only to preach a gospel of work, but to live up to it. I can never be sufficiently grateful to a kind Providence for sending, just at this juncture, in the affairs of this little State, *Waterboer*, with his indefatigable industry, to add weight to my teaching and example, which he nobly did. He was always at it; hardly ever would he be seen lolling about or wasting time. The preaching of this gospel of industry was thus supported by king and priest. We became fast friends. I found him intelligent, sober, honest, good. He acknowledged that the taste for liquor had laid its hold on him; that it had largely been created by the attentions and solicitations of the European friends, who had each an axe to grind. I never saw him the worse of liquor, but occasionally he was somewhat hilarious. The craving for drink, however, gradually grew upon him after his return to Griqualand West. He returned a few months before "annexation." He sent me, as a keepsake, three beautiful and valuable diamonds, which were stolen from my cabin in the s.s. the "*Edinburgh Castle*," on the voyage to England in 1877.

About this time, *Charles Bristey* erected his house of sod on the site now occupied by Mr. Dold's store. *E. Stafford* erected the wood structure, recently used as a boarding-house, and opened a store therein, which was conducted by Mr. Dixon, now Episcopal minister at Mount Ayliff. Most of the Griqua houses, of sod, and a few of them of brick, were run up about this time. By the beginning of 1874, there were, in all, about eighty houses dotted over the plain. To outsiders it will seem new and strange to speak of houses built of *sod*, and that by Europeans. Yet, in the early days of Kokstad, little else was dreamed of. Sod walls became an institution peculiar to the place. The first Government house had its walls of sod. Walls could be easily, cheaply, and quickly constructed of this material, which was abundant, ready to hand, and the best of its kind. A skilful workman could make sod walls strong and straight. When they were carefully plastered, whitewashed outside, and papered inside, they resembled the best brick wall. But woe to the peace of the occupants after the rats and mice had had time to burrow their tunnels and build their nests inside of them! At first all erven were enclosed by walls of sod. If well built and kept in repair they formed an excellent, though anything but a beautiful fence. If neglected they became extremely unsightly. In most cases the Griquas neglected their fences, and hence the town presented a ragged, ruined, repulsive, and desolate appearance, often provoking the remark, "The town ought to be called Sodville or the City of Sods"

While Goodliffe and Balance conducted business in the old Laager, the Griquas were gradually moving away from it. Their manager, Mr. W. Darby, was not at all sanguine about the removal ever taking place. He established a weekly post by Kaffir runner to the nearest post office in Natal. It was a private postal service, but practically became public *by having its own postage stamp.* This was the first attempt at a regular postal service If the Griqua Government wished to avail itself of the "*Mount Currie Express,*" it required to procure stamps, and use these, like anyone else There are, I am informed, by competent authority, four of the *Mount Currie Express* stamps preserved in the British Museum. If any others exist they would, no doubt, be quoted at a high figure in the market of stamp collectors. A notice of the history of this rare stamp, by Mr. Darby, appeared in the *Philatelists Journal,* but I do not know the date of the issue containing it. The picture of the stamp may be seen in page 15, part 3, of Stanley Gibbons Local Postage Stamps of the World, 1899, and an illustration will be found in another page. Much sooner than was expected, the Laager was deserted, and *Messrs. Goodliffe* and *Balance* found that they had to move also. The business left them; the store tumbled down; the doors and windows, and fittings, and timber, were bought up by the Rev. Mr. Kirkby, and used in the erection of a sod house, at the corner opposite the Congregational Manse. This house thus enjoys the distiuction of having in its structure the oldest articles of house furniture in Kokstad. It links the town on to the older settlement.

CHAPTER XI.

About the beginning of 1874, through the help of *Mr. Hutton,* of Bedford, who, later, became Hon. Treasure-General of the Colony, a sum of £1310, had been recovered from the miserable wreck of the Griqua Church properties, and the work of church building was resumed. The work was done almost entirely by Griqua labour, under my own personal superintendence. A good industrial training in early life proved of unspeakable value to me, in our isolated position. There were not many things of ordinary handicraft I could not do; but one thing baffled me. We had no blacksmith in Kokstad. The chisels for cutting the corners of our building stone required sharpening. I attempted this work myself, at the Government smithy, but miserably failed In the end, I had to send these tools, every other week, by pack horse, down to *Archie Scott,* near to Riet Vley. For any blacksmith's work required to be done on the spot, we used charcoal, burnt in Mt. Currie bush, but when that was not obtainable, we bought imported coal from the shops at the rate of *1-lb. of coal for the price of one acre of land.* The Griqua workmen engaged on the work had to be fed. Those who know the fastidiousness and capacity of the people, in the matter of food, will understand what sorrows and heart-burnings would attend the daily feeding of some fifteen workmen. The supreme difficulty, for a long time, was to get wheat *ground* Wheat was plentiful, and cheap, but the grinding cost as much as the purchase price. "Two women grinding at the mill" did not minister to economy or good temper. The meal difficulty seemed, at one time, insuperable I appealed to the Chief, hoping to be able to persuade him to erect a mill. "No," he said, "I built a mill at *Philipolis*, and the people seemed to expect me to grind their wheat for nothing. I won't build another" I appealed to Mr Brisley. "No; he would have nothing to do with mill property." The Chief said, "If you can construct a mill yourself, or can get one made, you may have any water right in the country which is not already allotted. I accepted that offer, selected a water power from the Mount Currie Spruit, and got title for it. I had a water leading, and a mill constructed. The latter I constructed myself, and, verily, it was fearfully and wonderfully made. I believe the kind of mill goes by the name of "Norse" mill. I had seen one at work in the Shetland Islands Its peculiarity is that the driving wheel revolves horizontally, and is driven not by the weight of water, acting like a lever, but purely by the force of the water striking against the mechanism. There is no multiplication of speed, a single revolution of the driving wheel making a single revolution of the grinding stone. It ground one bucketful in twenty-four hours; but once started, it required no attention, and it solved the bread difficulty. The site of this primitive structure was about three hundred yards below the drift of the old Natal road across the Mount Currie Spruit, east of the town. By-and-bye, I replaced this mill by another, with overshot wheel, cog wheel, spindle, and sifting apparatus. There was some excitement in the little town when the larger mill on the same site was set agoing, and it was found that it could convert 2 muids of wheat into very good boer meal every day. I had expended time and strength and patience on this bit of primitive machinery, and I confess that I felt a little bit proud of my achievement. This second mill supplied meal for the church building work, for my own family, and for the country side. Arthur Barker became miller. He ground free for the church, myself, and the Chief, charged all others, and made the thing pay him. The water right passed into the hands of *John Hill*, and the little mill thereafter went to Matatiela, where it did good, useful, work till our Colonial troops, during the Basuto war, chopped it to pieces for fuel to cook their food. When the church was completed, I sold the mill rights to John Hill, for the sum of £40. and the machinery of the mill for £25. These sums helped to defray the cost of a visit to the Old Country in 1877.

Early in the seventies, a question was raised as to the extent of the *commonage*, and there was a little unpleasantness before the question was finally set at rest. The farm on which Kokstad is situated originally belonged to *Martinus Davids*. He took up the farm with the full understanding that if the Government, at any time, required it for a township he would have to move elsewhere, *without compensation*. *Martinus* laughed at the idea of the Griquas ever building a town. and confidently had begun to build, enclose, and cultivate. When his farm was fixed on as the site, he received due notice, but declined to accept it intimating his purpose to bide his time, and seek for what he called his "*rights*" He continued his farming as if nothing had happened, and no one disturbed him. When the Chief and most members of the old Raad were dead, and after the Colonial Government had been formally established, then Martinus pressed his claim for *compensation*. After much negotiation and correspondence, extending over some years, Martinus had to be satisfied without any money compensation. He received a grant of land wherever he might choose to select his homestead, retaining his enclosed lands and pasture rights on the commonage. The transaction was all in his favour, but he grumbled, and went grumbling to his grave. To return to the question of *commonage*. It resolved itself into this. Is the farm of Davids and the adjoining veldt of William Bezuidenhout, and the southern face of Mount Currie sufficient? Some said "yes," others "nay," and there was considerable dissension over it. *Edward Barker* (who, meantime, had become surveyor), and myself, contended strongly for increased *commonage*. The Chief tried to be neutral, and Mr. Brisley also, though we knew that they leaned to our side. The farm to the west of Mount Currie, and north of the town, belonged to *Jan Bergover*, the Government Treasurer. He was a "man o' wecht" in the Privy Council, and he had, as his life-long friend, *Jan Jood* the Chief's son-in-law, whose daughter had come to be looked on by the family as the presumptive successor to the chieftianship. Jood and Bergover were good, worthy men, and had great influence. We urged that Bergover's grant should be cancelled, a double grant, if needful, given to him elsewhere, and his farm added to the commonage. Without this farm there would have been a perpetual grievance. At last Jan gave way, the friction passed, and the farm was added to the Town Lands.

The contention was short, but sharp, while it lasted. I expressed my opinion freely, and, for a time, incurred the displeasure of *Jan Bergover*, whose good opinion I valued as much as that of any man in the country. Kokstad owes more to the late *Edward Barker* than to any other man for the acquisition of its splendid commonage. He never rested till he had the boundaries fixed as they now are.

CHAPTER XII.

During the years which had passed since Kok occupied the country, his relations with the surrounding tribes had been, on the whole, pacific. With *Faku*, the old renowned and powerful Pondo chief, he was in friendly intercourse till his death. Deeds, dignified by the name of *treaties*, had been drawn and ratified between them, An unfortunate feud, however, had sprung up between the Griquas and *Makaula*, the Chief of the Amabacca, located around Mount Frere Uncertainty existed as to the exact boundary-line between them, near to the Umzimvubu Poort and beyond "*Nungi Neck*" On the debatable land there lived a petty chief, who was a famous cattle lifter, *Neukana* by name. He helped himself freely and frequently to the stock of Kok's subjects, Griqua, Kaffir, and Basuto. Such, at least, was the common accusation against him. Kok held that this offender was on the Baca side of the line, that Baca subjects aided and abetted him in concealing the stolen property so far inside the Baca territory that there could be no question of boundary. Makaula would neither restrain the thief nor restore the stolen property. Kok's patience became exhausted, he declared war, and called out his burghers. "*Rooi Jan*" *Pienaar*, a Griqua of the purest blood, was appointed Commandant. Under *Rooi Jan* was placed *Lodowijk Kok* and *Adam Johannes Kok*, familiarly known as "*Adam Muis*," an arrangement which at once created a grievance with these two "princes of the blood." Rooi Jan came into prominence now for the first time. When the war was over he retired into the obscurity from which he ought never to have emerged. He had all the characteristics of a Griqua,—an expert horseman, a crack shot, built in the prodigality of nature, amazingly self possessed, imperious, haughty, dignified proud and penniless;—"a gentleman of broken means." Jan took command of some 300 burghers; most of them rode good horses, and were well provided with fire-arms and ammunition, vastly superior to the style of fire-arm obtaining among the Kaffirs at that time. These were mostly old tower muskets or gas pipes, skilfully manipulated into a cheap fire-arm. Whether due to superior skill, or superior arms, or force of stricter discipline, I know not, but in a couple of weeks Rooi Jan was dictating terms to Makaula, almost at his Kraal gate. A fine of, I think, 700 head of cattle was imposed and enforced. Negotiations followed, issuing in the removal of the cause of offence from the border. The distribution of the captured stock and fine led to heart burnings, jealousy, and strife, which, in my humble opinion, was more deplorable than all Neukaua's depredations.

This little war had an important bearing on the future of Griqualand East. Makaula, and those who sympathized with him, called the attention of the Cape Government to the necessity for investigation and the defining of the boundaries. Responsible government had been established at the Cape, and *Charles Brownlee* was Secretary for Native Affairs. The anomalous position of Kok and his Griquas had not escaped his attention. The Natal Government too, which had from the first, claimed priority of right to *Nomansland*, and had looked with no friendly eye on the semi independent and semi civilized state which had been planted on her borders, called on the Cape to look after her unruly children or proteges more closely.

About this time another event served to draw the attention of the new Government to the Griqua position. Mr. T. O. Hall kept a small business in the Laager, or rather the business kept him; he had become a *persona ingrata* with the Government, particularly with *Lodowijk Kok*, because he, Hall, had refused to give to the Government unlimited credit. Lodowijk declined to give any security for the payment of goods ordered, except the word of the Magistrate, and said that as Hall held a Griqua licence for trading in the country, he was bound to sell in good faith, to the order of its officers. This I think was the real root of the strife, but the immediate *occasion* was Hall's demurring to the payment of a heavy fine for the use of a weight alleged to be false. Hall declined to do business on their terms. Next day after their epistolary tussle, wagons were commandeered by *Lodowijk* *Hall's* goods, furniture, and family were unceremoniously loaded up and, *nolens volens,* he and his belongings were conveyed to the Natal boundary, and off-loaded at the spot where the *Ingeli Hotel* and trading post now stands, and left there on the open veldt, to shift as best they could. Mr. Hall was next to ruined, for having no *locus standi* in the country, and having incurred the displeasure of the "Groote menschen" he could not easily recover outstanding debts. He began to trade on the spot where he had been set down, on which the brothers Scott had traded for some time before, and there bided his time. We shall afterwards see how "the whirligig of time brings its revenges."

These high handed proceedings did not meet the approval of the more intelligent of the Griqua burghers, nor, indeed, did the chief himself approve; the thing was done before he had the chance of interfering.

This illustrates, what I have elsewhere noticed, the over-lapping of the judicial authority, and functions, which prevailed within this miniature state. Hall reported his case to Cape Town, and questions asked in the House of Parliament attracted the attention of the country to the anomalous state of affairs. After a lapse of about two years, *Kok* made compensation to *Hall*, granted him business stands in the new town, to which he came back in triumph, and succeeded in establishing a prosperous business.

CHAPTER XIII.

The question had often been raised who would succeed *Adam Kok*. There was a "*William Kok*," familiarly known as "*Tol*" He was the son of Mrs Kok, but the accident of his paternity excluded him from all claim. There were several heirs "presumptive." The *Jood* family, the *Eta* family, the *Waterboer* family each set up claims and candidates. Some of the *apprentices* or slave descendents ventured to argue that, seeing *Adam Kok I.* had been himself an escaped slave, a representative of that class might well be selected to sit in the Kaptyn's seat, and hold his staff of office. The *Waterboer* and *Jood* families had concocted a plan by which their respective claims might be united by the marriage of Waterboer's eldest son to Jood's daughter. There was no Salic law in force, but there was no precedent of a Griqua *Chieftainess* bearing rule among their people. Precedent had almost the force of law.

The prejudice against the idea of a Queen ruling had been at one time very strong, and when hopes of issue from the union of A. *Kok III.* with his deceased brother's widow failed, then *Adam Kok* as good as adopted the eldest son of his cousin, *Adam Eta Kok*, familiarly known as "*Eta*." The boy lived in the Chief's house, and was taught to think of himself as the "*heir apparent*." He accompanied *Kok* and his Councillors to Cape Town in 1868, woed there a bride, and was married in right royal style When this wife died, he returned to Cape Town and married her cousin. Meantime the "*Eta Kok*" influence began to decline, and that of *Jood* increased. The illustrious reign of QUEEN VICTORIA had familiarized *Kok* with the idea of a woman succeeding him. "Why not?" Jood was his wife's son in-law, Jood's daughter was growing up, handsome, amiable, and, in a moderate way, accomplished. She was the grandchild of Kok's immediate predecessor (his elder brother), and so his own niece along the line of primogeniture, and, besides, the child of his own adopted daughter. I have already mentioned the arrival of *Waterboer*, and his stay in the Laager, from 1872 to '74. He, too, was Kok's stepson-in-law. *Waterboer's* eldest son, by marrying his cousin, Jood's eldest daughter, would unite the candidature of the two families to reign together. This, certainly, looked like that "tide in the affairs of men which, taken at the flood, leads on to fortune"—a lasting *Kok-Waterboer* dynasty—a waking dream that seemed all natural, and likely enough.

Alas! When the time for the projected overtures arrived, it was found that the marriage proposals had to be abandoned, for reasons which well-nigh broke the hearts of the girl's parents, and made every patriotic and respectable Griqua hang his head with shame and sorrow. Verily, one sinner destroyeth much good.

Little was said openly, yet a good deal of secret controversy went on as to the "succession." "Division smouldered hidden," partisanship was strong, and even perilous. Had *Adam Kok* died suddenly at any time between 1869 and '74, his death would have been the signal for civil strife, and it would have led to much bloodshed.

All these things—the Baca war, the undefined boundaries, the making of treaties, inflicting of capital punishment, Hall's case, the possible strife over succession, and a good deal more, were known to the new Secretary for Native Affairs.

A Commission was appointed to proceed to *Nomans'and* to investigate and report. The three Commissioners were *Colonel* (then *Mr.*) *Griffith*, *Colonel* (then *Inspector*) *Grant*, and *James Ayliffe, Esq*. All three are still alive, but retired on pension. For a week they sat under the verandah of the old shop in the Laager, taking voluminous evidence on all the subjects already mentioned, excepting the question of succession. That was the subject of private discussion with the chief This Commission was the first indication to *Kok* that his action and position were receiving the serious attention of the Government. Sir Philip Woodhouse had visited him a few years before, just after concluding the Aliwal Convention, but the only issue of the visit was an extension of territory and the verbal commission: "*Do the best you can ; we will not interfere with you.*"

These Commissioners lodged with us in the unfinished Parsonage, and proceeded daily to the Laager to listen to the interminable talk from Griquas, Bacas, Pondos, Basutos. All they said, in the six days' talking, might have been well said in the course of a single forenoon. But this is the native way—"*Een mensch moet praat, alla wereld!!*"

Almost immediately after this Commission had sent in its report, *Joseph M. Orpen*, now Surveyor-General for Rhodesia, was appointed *British Resident* for the whole of the Transkei, including Kok's country. He took up his residence on the banks of the *Tsitsa*, not far from the present Mount Fletcher. He was to be "*the eyes and ears and mouthpiece of the Government*" to all the surrounding tribes. I do not think I am misjudging Mr. Orpen when I say that *he did not like the Griquas*. Against them he had an unreasonable and invincible prejudice. They were to him evil, only evil, and evil continually. He was a strong partisan of the Basutos, and contended, with almost reckless disregard of Griqua interests and facts, that the whole "*Griqua country ought to belong to the Basutos*" The Griquas, of course, soon found out how Orpen was disposed towards them, and there was no love lost between him and them. He kept worrying *Kok* with a ceaseless flow of bombastic despatches on every miserable trifle. He went to the very extreme of his authority to belittle Kok—a treatment which the Chief bitterly resented, and which, with all his faults, he did not deserve. *Mr. Brisley*, though still officially Government Secretary, had moved his residence from *Kokstad* to Umzimkulu. He had become a partner in the firm *Strachan and Co.*, and only visited Kokstad about once a month. The Chief had to depend on very imperfect Griqua clerical assistance in the intervals of *Brisley's* visits. It thus came about that, for a time, perhaps about six months, I had, frequently, to advise the Chief, and do a good part of his correspondence. I did not like this, because I have a strong conviction that it is wise for ministers and missionaries, as far as possible, to refrain from interfering in the politics of the country in which they are located. Orpen was a personal friend, and stayed with me, during his frequent visits to Kokstad. While sympathising with his desire to see a firmer Government established, I disapproved of his spirit, and not a few of his methods; and, on the other hand, while not championing all Kok's doings, I sympathised with his feeling of honest pride and self-respect, which seemed to be unnecessarily trampled on by the action of the Resident.

Let me here try and briefly place before my readers the facts which, during the winter months of 1874, seemed to rankle in the old man's mind. He had been abandoned by the Government in the *Bloemfontein Convention*, betrayed by the *Secret Treaty*, and by the refusal to allow ammunition. Practically he had been handed over to the tender mercies of the Dutch Boers, to be obliterated bit by bit, root and branch, and all this in spite of treaty obligations, declared to be still in force. He had come into the new country, much against his will, as a British subject, with the promise of magisterial help. That had failed him. He had been told to govern his people, and rule the country as best he could. He had done it. He had become used to his independence. His people had begun to think and speak of themselves again as a Volk, a Nation. Very rightly, he now resented this pin-pricking, and the limitations implied in Mr. Orpen's appointment and the imperious tone of his despatches. Beyond all doubt, Orpen's policy and objective, if not indeed his fad, was *annexation*. I believe that even against that, Kok would not have objected, for he was conscious of the anomalous character of his position. But he had the conviction that he was being hounded and worried from the quarter from which he ought to get help, advice, guidance, and sympathy. Had he not opened up that new country? Without making roads, had he not found out the best and most passable tracks? If he had not built bridges, had he not found passable drifts? Had he not cleared the country of wild beasts, and demonstrated its fitness for agricultural and pastoral industries? Had he not done all the rough pioneer work, without the protection of a single soldier, or the expenditure of a single shilling of Colonial or Imperial money? Had he not founded a township and established organised Government, which, with all its defects, was far in advance of anything attempted by any Kaffir or Basuto tribe? Had he not given his people title to their holdings—a first step to a higher civilisation? If they abused their privileges, let them suffer for their folly. Thus Kok argued, and was he not quite right? He declined to be treated as if he was a barbarous heathen, and I, for one, hold he did right.

Events soon occurred elsewhere which favoured Orpen's scheme of annexation, and brought matters to a crisis.

Langa'ibilele rebelled in Natal, and took refuge in the Drakensberg mountains. A section of the same *Hlubi* tribe was settled near Kok's country, and their chief, *Zibe*, was the intimate friend and blood relation of the rebel chief. It was, naturally, surmised that he would try to make his way through the Maluti mountains, to join his relative, who would then make common cause with him, and spread the spirit of insubordination. It was said that there was evidence of intrigue, and correspondence between the two, and, indeed, that messages of a somewhat mysterious character had been passing to and fro among other chiefs and tribes in the Transkei. To check this possible movement, the Natal Government invited Kok to assist with a Griqua levy. In twenty-four hours Kok had mounted men on their way over the flats to the appointed rendezvous. The rapidity and promptitude of the response to Kok's call to arms excited admiration and gratitude. The Veld-cornets rode all night from farm to farm, and roused the sleeping Burghers While the men got the horses from the veldt and saddled them, the women put into the saddle-bags the available provender—coffee, sugar, and tobacco. A hunch of biltong was hung at the side, also a tin pannikin, and in front was fastened the blanket—all this the work of an hour, and the Griqua was off full tilt to the meeting-place of his particular ward.

This little Griqua army discharged the service asked for satisfactorily, and, I believe, free of charge to Government The combined force checked the southward movement of the rebels, and drove the Hlubi into the arms of Colonel Griffith, in Basutoland.

Mr Orpen now found from this a new text, from which to preach "*Annexation*," which was his favourite theme "Do you not see," he said, "that until such time as you annex the whole territory, stretching from the one Colony to the other, and from the Drakensberg to the sea, *you will always have a land vacuum*, which will offer a possible asylum for discontented and dangerous spirits. At this nail in the coffin of Griqua independence he hammered vigorously, in his despatches to Government and Reports to Parliament. He might have summed up his case in the simple statement that John Bull, like Nature, abhors a vacuum, in the possession of the earth.

GRIQUA CHURCH, KOKSTAD.

MR. EDWARD BARKER.

CHAPTER XIV.

During the winter months of 1874, Orpen was in Kokstad The late Bishop of St. John's, then *Rev. Barnabas Key*, accompanied him, and both were guests in my home. There was some plain speaking between the Chief and *Orpen* I was, happily, out of it this time, for *Mr. Brisley* had come up from Umzimkulu. The echoes of this strife of tongues, however, reached me. Kok said something like this : " Mr. Orpen, " you have, I know, doubted my loyalty. I am grateful for the " opportunity, recently given me, of demonstrating that I am " not the disloyal man you would represent me to be. If my " Burghers are required at any time to help in maintaining the " Queen's Supremacy they will always be ready I now wish " to have my position defined. Ever since I have come to this " new country, I have asked for this. I ask it again. If I am " an independent chief, leave me a free hand, along with my " people, to manage our little state in our own way, so long as " I do not injure others, or damage Colonial interests. If I " am not an independent chief, then beg of the Government " for me, to carry out the original condition of our settlement, " and relieve me of responsibility. I am too old to be kept in " hot water like this any longer." I venture to think there was sound reason and good policy in what the old man said.

In the following September, *Sir Arthur Cunningham*, General in Command at the Cape, and his suite, passed through Kokstad, and stayed the best part of a week with us at the Parsonage. He seemed to take a lively interest in the affairs of the little State. He had frequent informal interviews with the Chief. One of them was of a more formal and courtly character. The General was invited to *afternoon tea* at the " Palace." He went in full uniform—cocked hat, waving feathers, dangling sword, military gloves, " with all his honours on his breast," his aide-de camp, likewise, in shining array. It fell to me, as his host, to accompany him. We walked in procession, between a double line of mounted burghers, from the Parsonage to the " Palace." There Adam Smith, a well-known Kokstad character, in somewhat faded and mixed uniform, mounted guard at the door, and presented arms, with more loyalty than grace. Inside, all the heads of departments, including the cook and the herd boy, were assembled. *Wenzel Hemroe*, long known in Kokstand, as Interpreter of the Court, acted in that capacity at this time. The " ladies of the household " were also present, and the younger of them served coffee and substantial refreshments The formalities were tiresome and grotesque ; the conversation was, at first, desultory and embarrassing, for the Griquas had an idea that the General had some special commission up his sleeve. After sundry, somewhat dry remarks about the weather, the health of the family, the course of the General's journey, its destination, and other such generalities, the ice was gradually broken, and the frigidity passed away, when something like the following conversation took place: ' Chief, why don't you make better roads? Roads are the first steps to civilisation, and needful to progress. The first thing the old Romans did was to make good roads, when they went into a new country." "I suppose these Romans were white people, like you, and not coloured, like us" "Oh, yes, they were white." "Ay! I thought so; if they had been coloured they would have known better. The fact is, our roads are too good already, and if we make them better, the white men will come in and buy up all the land, and then what would the roads profit us?" "Chief, your town is beautifully situated, and well laid out, but I do not see any provision made for a *Park and Public Garden*. You should attend to that as soon as possible." "What, General! a *Park* and a *Garden*, like that I saw in Cape Town? General, you don't know this country, nor do you know the weaknesses of our people. Garden! park! Oh, no; the trees would bring the birds. the birds would eat the ripe corn, and we would have no bread! The shade, too, would be so nice; my people would want to sit under it all day long, instead of cultivating their farms, and by-and-bye they would be beggars. No, General! we must 'wacht een beetje' for these nice things."

These are snatches of the conversation held on this State occasion.

The reader will find an extended description of the General's visit to *Nomansland* and *Kokstad*, and also of his stay with the writer, in a book which he afterwards published, entitled, "*My Command in South Africa*," chapter xvi. Macmillan, 1879.

CHAPTER XV.

On the 15th October, 1874, we received from the Chief a message to say that the Governor, *Sir Henry Barkly*, and his staff, would arrive in Kokstad next day, and that he, the Chief, was depending on us for accommodation. A cavalcade of Griqua Burghers, headed by *Adam Eta*, had gone out to meet and escort His Excellency. But about five o'clock, in the twilight, came a second message to say that *Sir Henry* was on his way, and would arrive in about half-an-hour. The new appointment upset all domestic arrangements, and plunged the commissariat and culinary departments of my home into agitation and dismay. My wife hurriedly put the children to bed, only to find them subsequently scrambling on the window sill, to hear the salute, and soon after His Excellency's arrival, to find our small boy, now the minister of the Congregational Presbyterian Church, Queenstown, sitting on Sir Henry's knee before the dining-room fire absorbed in strictly private and confidential communications from the extraordinary visitor, tired though he was, after a very rough-and-tumble journey. Outside, all was commotion. Every soul in the place was assembled fo see the great man.

"The little village, all astir,
Now turned out, to a man, to greet him;
And ragged urchins, wide agape,
Ran down the dusty road to meet him."

Mr. Orpen, and his clerk, *Mr, Gladwin*, had come from the opposite direction, to meet the Governor.

Next morning, *Sir Henry* and *Mr. Orpen* were closeted in my study, and then and there they formulated the conditions on which annexaton should take place.

By twelve o'clock (16th October), the Chief, his Council, and the people had filled the schoolroom and surrounding verandahs. From the Parsonage, a kind of gubernatorial procession was marshalled. First, went four F.A.M.P., under command of a sergeant; then *Sir Henry*, in Windsor uniform, and wearing several decorations, beside him, I found myself, as Sir Henry's host, and the sole representative of ecclesiastical authority in the place; then followed Sir Henry's Secretary and his aide-de-camp; then Mr. Orpen and Mr Gladwin; then a company of the F A.M.P., under command of Inspector O'Connor. We marched round to the place of meeting, through double lines of mounted Griqua Burghers. Arrived at the Schoolroom, the Governor addressed the Chief and the crowd very briefly, every word being translated into Dutch. The following is the substance of what he said: "The Government "believes that the time has come when it is advisable to "relieve *Adam Kok* of the responsibilities of the office he has "filled so long and so well. His age and the circumstances "of the country seem to demand this. The Government has, "therefore, decided to assume, from to day, the administration "of the affairs of this territory. Suitable provision will be made "for the Chief, and allowances will also be made for the "members of his *Council*. All bona-fide titles to land will be "confirmed. All other claims for land, by the Griquas, will be "generously dealt with. Mr. Orpen will now read to you the "conditions."

These conditions were as follows:—

1.—Captain Adam Kok shall continue to hold his present honorary title, and will receive a fixed salary, which shall amount, together with the allowances that he presently receives, from the Colonial and Imperial Governments, to £1000 per annum, in consideration of his past services and his position, as President of a Council, whose functions will be defined by Goyernment, and of such assistance as Government will require of him, in arranging the affairs of the country.

2.—The present Government officials will remain in their present position, and receive their present salaries, until Government can acquaint itself with their cases and qualifications, and it can be decided which can remain or receive some fair retiring allowance.

3.—The present laws will remain in force, until Government can acquaint itself with them, and their suitability and the wishes of the Captain, and the people will receive fair consideration whenever expressed.

4.—Titles to land will remain in their present position, until after due inquiry, they are confirmed by Government, which will deal justly and liberally with them.

5.—All Government property, and all documents, connected with the Government business, in Old and New Griqualand, will be handed to the British Resident, or those appointed by him, upon application.

6.—All just debts of the present Government will be liquidated by means of arrears and incoming revenue.

7.—The government of the country, for the future, will be carried on under instruction, by the British Resident, Joseph Millerd Orpen, Esq.

N.B.—The above is a true copy.

When *Mr Orpen* had finished, and these conditions had been translated into Dutch, he sat down, and there was silence, long and painful. I shall never forget the looks of anxiety, almost amounting to terror, depicted on the faces around me that day. Some of them indicated disappointment and ill-concealed anger. A few there were who gnashed their teeth. At last the Chief, who was suffering from a severe cold, and had sat, head on hands, elbows on knees, gave his wonted and familiar grunt, looked up, and said: "*Daar het jille dit nu*" "There you are, now." Again silence, at last broken by the Chief, who, still sitting, said, "*Governor, this has come suddenly.* "*We were not consulted. We can say nothing. We ask the* "*Governor to give us time for consultation, and to meet us again* "*later in the day*" This, of course, was granted, and we marched back to my house in the same order and dignified formality.

There was no small excitement among the Griquas that afternoon. They stood in groups discussing the situation. A very few expressed satisfaction—disappointed litigants and a few irreconcilables. With these exceptions, consternation and perplexity were stamped on every face.

The proposed afternoon meeting never took place, although *Mr. Brisley* had a brief interview with the *Governor* and *Mr. Orpen.* The conditions were subsequently modified, but only in a few unimportant particulars.

Thus ended this simple, brief, historical, ceremony of "*annexation.*" It put a stop, almost at once, to a good deal of objectionable favouritism and nepotism, and some hoary mal-practices, which sprang more from the miserable weakness of the central authority than from any actual and intentional dishonesty. People who valued justice, equality, impartiality, and fair play, breathed more freely. This act increased, at once, and by fourfold, the value of every foot of land in the territory : it opened the door for capital and industry. Did the Griquas view it in that light? By no means. To hint at benefits likely to follow the "*annexation*" was to be regarded as a traitor to their "self-standigheid." They became sullen and irritated. Even those who had secretly longed for the change cried out bitterly against the way in which it had been effected. The "*oerneeming*"—"*annexation*" created a *new grievance*, and, as I have said elsewhere, the average Griqua of those days was not happy unless he had a grievance. To many it was a complete justification for spending ten out of every twenty-four hours in talk. It is much easier to talk over grievances than to hoe mealies or plant potatoes ; "*Mensch moet praat alla wereld !*" ("One must talk.")

The head and front of the offending lay in this, that they had not been consulted. There had been no "vergaderings," no "praat," no treaty, no diplomacy. They had been "*taken over like so many cattle or sheep.*" "They were not livestock," "or Kaffirs," or "onbeschafed," or "helots," but "Burghers of a State," "a people," "a natie." To the use of all these lofty titles, which, in the more enlightened, excite a smile, they had become thoroughly accustomed, and felt no incongruity in the use of them. Right well do I know that the Cape Government, and especially the *Hon Charles Brownlee*, to whose department this matter belonged, meant no harm or even disrespect to the Griquas ; the very opposite. Certain it is that annexation had saved them from civil strife, and opened up, to the very poorest among them, possibilities and opportunities otherwise unattainable. But these people were blinded by prejudice, ignorance, and pride. For months one heard of nothing but the "*oerneeming.*" A failure of crops, an untimely frost, a destructive storm, a sudden death, a maternal disappointment, were all, by some of the more ignorant, attributed to the "*oerneeming.*" Appeals to reason, common-sense, or even a prudent use of satire, were always met by the question, "How would you like to be treated like beasts, and have to change your allegiance by the stroke of a pen, without being asked by your leave" ?

It was, beyond all question, a huge mistake to trample on the feelings, and prejudices, and tender toes, of a whole people, by the summary process adopted. A Dutch-speaking agent of the stamp of the present Chief Magistrate, *J. Scott, Esq.*, or a man like the late *C. P. Watermeyer*, conversant with their prejudices and language, sent up to spend a month in harmless talk, innocent diplomacy, and formal treaty-making might have brought off *annexation*, with flags flying and trumpets blowing Forcing it on them, without recognising their semi-independence, for the maintenance of which we had made ourselves responsible, set the match to all the explosive elements of their composition. The difference would have been the difference between contented and discontented subjects, between confidence and rooted suspicion. The Griquas have inherited, through the Boer blood, which runs in their veins, much of the Boer love of independence, his prejudice against any too heavy touch of the hand of government upon his individual freedom, his dogged headstrong "*thrawnness*" which has taxed the resources of our diplomacy, the skill and force of British arms.

I doubt, very much, if all the diplomacy and bargaining in the world would have prevented the bulk of the Griquas from selling their farms. "Easy come, easy go," is a proverb which embodies a comprehensive principle. But I am convinced that some wise, conciliatory action, of the kind I have indicated, would have shut the mouths of Griquas, who, being determined to sell, found a salve to their consciences and an excuse to their fellows, in the alleged bad faith of the Government.

Here I am tempted, if not to scale Parnassus, at least to invoke the aid of the Muses, who condescend to convey inspiration through the medium of the Taal.

GRIQUA KLAAG-LIED VAN DE OVERNEEMING.

KOKSTAD, 16th October, 1874.

Oom David! het je wat gehcor?
Ons Griqas het de land verloor,
De Engelsman, nu staat ons voor.
Ons . . uitgeschop.

Neef Hans! is dat toch mogelijk?
Ik voel als of ik moet bezwijk,
Dat iemand van ons Koningrijk.
Die kroon afzet.

'T's waar 't's waar, ik was aldaar,
Go'rneur en Orpen—slimme paar!!
Maak' toover-broodjes zoet en gaar,
Om veld te win.

Oom Klaas, broer Jan en vader Jood,
Bekommerd hen op dagelijks brood.
Een lekker maand-ge'd tot den dood,
Stellt hul gerust.

Kaptijn krijgt jaarlijks DUIZEND-POND!
Dat smeert hem zuiker op de mond.
En ons betaal voor kat en hond.
En krijgt . . net nix.

Dit ruwe land het ons regeer,
De Engelsh speelde mooi weer,
Nu vangt hij Griqua, net's een dier,
Wil hij, of niet.

Als 't muizen is de slag van kat,
De Engelsh slag is grond te vat,
Een spijker het hij voor elk gat,
En drijft hem in.

Zet hij een planje op de touw,
Wat veld te win, al is 't hoe naauw,
Dan schudt hul geld toch uit de mouw,
En neemt hem in.

Nu moet ons met de OU VROUW praat,
Zij was toch lang Kaptiju's 'e maat,
Te weten is't of dat zal baat,
Maar laat's probeer.

CHAPTER XVI.

The Cape Government had now "assumed the administration of the affairs of the country." Popularly this was termed "annexation." In point of fact it was not annexation. The *conditions* referred to no authority under which the action was taken. They did not even bear a signature. So far as I can discover, they did not appear in print until next year's Blue Book was published. The Supreme Court had no jurisdiction, the Queen's writ could not legally run. Annexation took place in 1879.

Before proceeding to describe the events which followed the 16th October, '74, let us take a look at Kokstad as it then was.

At this date the place was a mere hamlet. Counting the ordinary Griqua sod-dwelling a house, there were, in all, about fifty houses. The *Parsonage* was the first built, and the largest. Next in time and size came *Adam Kok's* house, or "The *Palace*," as it came to be called, half in joke half in earnest. Next came the house in which the *Kokstad Advertiser* is now located, built by *Titus Klein*, a very respectable old slave man. *Mr Brisley's* house, where *Mr. Dold's* shop now stands. A blacksmith's shop stood on the site of the present post office. There was only one house above "the stony kopie—*Saunder's house*." It is still standing, close on the edge of the water furrow. There are a few relics of old Kokstad still left. The round hut at the N.W. corner of the Market Square is one. It was built by A. P. D. Smith, and the whole erf on which it stands, with Bank and shop-buildings, was his grant or town plot. The dining-room and kitchen attached to the house in which *Mrs. Barker* now lives, is one of the very oldest structures. The baker's shop, S.E. corner of the Square, was erected about 1873. The house now belonging to Mr. Dold, facing the Main Street, north side of the Congregational Church, was built in 1874. It is, for Griqualand East, an historical building. Here, *T. A. Cumming*, the successor of Orpen, and first Resident Magistrate, held his court. Here the Commission, and afterwards, for a time, the Land Court, held their sittings. Here Captain Blyth at first ruled. This house was the scene of many exciting meetings between officials and Griqua deputations. Another interesting relic is the house opposite the western gable of the Griqua Church. Here the "*Committee of Twelve,*" a political organisation, supposed to represent and be the mouthpiece of the Griqua people, held its monthly sittings. Here, in speeches long, loud, and threatening, but perfectly harmless, grievances, were discussed, petitions, memorials, etc., were drawn up. I always looked on these meetings as the safety valve of the Commonwealth. Some dogs there are which never bite as long as they can vent their energy in barking When the *Committee of Twelve* was prevented from meeting "*to praat,*" then matters became serious, and action commenced. *Captain Blyth* sat on the safety valve, and explosions followed.

There were two shops—*Stafford's*, in the wooden building opposite the Market Place, and *T. O. Hall's*, just above the Wesleyan Church T. O. H. had returned in triumph. Of religious edifices there was, 1st, the Griqua Schoolroom (The church walls were well up and getting ready for the roof). 2nd, a small Kaffir (Wesleyan) Church, at the S.W. corner of the Square, which afterwards bcame the dining-room of the Bank Manager. There was in the place neither Post nor Magistrates' Office, baker, nor butcher, shoemaker nor tailor, agent nor attorney, printer nor editor, policeman nor soldier, prison nor canteen, hotel nor lodging-house.

Adam Kok persisted in kraaling his cattle on the main street, opposite his house, It was very disgusting and trying to patience, the more so, seeing the town water furrow ran through it. There was no surveillance of the furrow, which often formed a temporary grave for poverty-stricken cattle in the winter months. Some progress had been made in inclosing erven and planting trees. The first *tree* planted was at the N.W. corner of my old garden, an almond tree. The planting took place in August, 1871, and was preceded by a brief religious service. The tree was held in position by my eldest daughter, whose mortal remains lie in the Congregational Cemetery. I believe there is only one man living, a Griqua, besides the members of my own family, who was present on that occasion—a little man called *William Plaatjes.* The large willow tree, at the opposite corner of the Parsonage ground, sprang from a piece of a branch about a foot long, and the thickness of a pencil, brought in September, 1871, from the farm of the late *Hans Berzuidenhout* Slips have gone from that tree to half the farms in the Mount Currie district. The first *oak* planted came from "*Cromwell,*" Umzimkulu, lashed to the disselboom of my wagon, about 1872, and stands, or stood, in front of the Parsonage. It is the parent of many a goodly tree in the district. The first *rose bush* in the town came from the front of the one house, which formed the nucleus of the town Stuartown Ixopo. The first child born in the town was my second son, J. M. Dower, now the minister of Trinity Church, Grahamstown.

Before leaving the old Griqua régime, with its comparative quiet and primitive ways. to the ferment of the faster life of the succeeding years, I am tempted to glance at a few of the men and women who were prominent characters in the town, and who may be regarded as types of their class. A sketch of the Chief Adam Kok will appear in a later chapter.

Kaptyn Kok's Wife.—She was the widow of *Abraham Kok*, Adam's elder brother. Before his decease, Adam supplanted him, and on his death married the widow, and adopted the three daughters. She was as pure a specimen of the Griqua woman as was then alive—olive complexion, short, woolly, peppercorn hair, sleepy eyes, high cheek bones, small hands. Her type of beauty was not exactly queenly, nor the sort that awakens the raphsodies of the poets. In truth, she was but a charred, wrinkled piece of womanhood.

"No ladies kissed Her Majesty's hand,
It was not the custom in Lillyput land."

Midway between the extremities, Nature had been extremely prodigal, so as to make walking neither easy nor graceful. This lady might have sat for a model to a Parisian dressmaker, without any artificial aids, in order to set forth the grotesque feminine disfigurement which the freaks of fashion made popular in the middle of the eighties. Had "Lady Kok" once walked along the Champs Elysées, in Paris, or Rotten Row, in London, the steel mills which were then running day and night, to assist in producing this horrible artificial excrescence might have all gone into liquidation at once. Lady Kok was not a scholar nor a linguist. Of English she knew nothing; of Dutch she knew only a little; but she spoke the old Griqua tongue to perfection. With her few female attendants, who were able to understand and speak with her, she was sociable and talkative. With all others, especially white people, she was shy and taciturn. Although she was a member of my church twenty years, I knew her no better at the end than at the beginning. She bore no children to *Adam Kok.* She seldom left her room, and I have no hesitation in saying that this African princess weakened her constitution and shortened her life by the wearing of excessive loads of body clothing, and by a chronic aversion to fresh air. Her eldest daughter was the wife of *Jan Jood*, perhaps the most influential member of the Chief's *Council*, and their daughter was, for long, regarded as the heir-apparent to the chieftainship. On the death of the Chief, she continued to exercise some influence with the tribe, for a little, but that gradually died out, and she became a nonentity in the public life of the place, up to the date of Captain Blyth's arrival. The events which followed, described elsewhere, brought her again prominently before the public. She continued to draw, till her death, £100 of the £200 payable to the Chief under the Smith Treaty. Her mortal remains lie in the vault beside those of her husband, and beneath what is dignified by the name of monument, in the centre of the town.

Cornelius Van der Westhuizen was father to the quondam Resident Magistrate, whose adventure with the future Premier of Natal is noted elsewhere. He was, from the time of his manhood, a Councillor—a member of the Upper House, a peer of the realm. He was of the bluest of blue Griqua blood. He was unlike a Griqua in that he was tall and stately, and walked erect, without slouching. He was a typical Griqua in that he was never known to do a stroke of work. I do not remember ever having seen him with an article of human industry in his hand. He was a typical Councillor, in that he saved himself a lot of needless thinking, secured his seat, and made sure of liberal pickings, by always saying "Yea" and "Amen" to whatever the Chief said. He was one of the very few men who could give evidence as to the exact *original* position of "*David's Graf*" on which question partly depended the conflicting claims of Great Britain and the Orange Free State to the rightful ownership of the diamond fields. He gave his evidence to Orange Free State Commissioners a few days after Adam Kok's death, but as it by no means supported the Orange Free State's claim, very likely it did not go to England to Earl Carnavon. Cornelius was signatory to the Power of Attorney, under which the Griqua Agent sold the residuary estate of the Griqua Government, and on which the Orange Free State founded its claims. He accompanied Adam Kok to Cape Town, in 1868, when the Chief went to meet the Governor to confer on matters of State, but especially to purchase cannon, that he might overawe the Kaffirs. Cornelius, done up in fashionable attire, crowned with a top hat, attracted the attention of the coloured folks in Cape Town, who looked on him as the *Prime Minister* of a great African prince, and obsequiously made their salaams to him. More than once he appeared in the rooms of Government House, as he said himself, with fear and trembling. He towered above Adam Kok head and shoulders, and, besides, had less colour in him. With many, colour and bulk is everything. Cornelius must needs bring home a present for his wife, who was one of the best women I ever knew, judged by the highest moral standards. A hymn-book, or a large print Bible would have been to her like hidden treasure, but a Councillor's present must be worthy of his dignity. So Cornelius must needs bring a fashionably made, expensive, sky-blue silk dress for his old dame. She was a wise woman, with a keen sense of decorum, and greeted the costly gift with the salutation, "Wat voor een ding voor een oud vrouw! Foei toch, Cornelius! jou is gek"—("What a thing for an old wife! Cornelius, you are an old fool!") Sundry operations with Tanta Metjes' scissors were necessary before she could get inside at all, and the courtly train was docked off, so as to rescue it from the indignity of sweeping the smeared floor, and made into capjes for the grandchildren. Cornelius vowed that he would never go a-shopping for his wife again. Poor fellow! he never again had the chance. Cornelius' religion was sound and sincere, as far as it went; but it was more negative than positive, passive than active. He never did much good, but he did no harm. Three days after Adam Kok's death he was elected by the *combined Raads provisional Kaptyn*. It meant little to Cornelius, and, as a matter of fact, little to others, for, by this time, Griqua patriotism had become largely extinct, and the chief concern was to secure grants of land. After annexation, he continued to draw his three pounds a month till his death, and this in compensation for lost dignity and pickings.

Smith Pommer.—This remarkable character left his mark on the country. Without scruple, I think I can say that he was ugly, positively repulsive. His face at once suggested the missing link, and some speculative theories of man's evolution from lower forms of life. He was a freak of Nature, or, possibly, a reversion to type. Smith began life in the Kat River Valley, and while still a youth, joined a company of Kat River rebel Hottentots in the war of 1850-51. Into his mad escapades this is not the place to go. Suffice it to say, that he showed himself then, to be what he ever after proved to be, a born leader of men. It came as naturally to this man to lead as a stag of ten, and, unfortunately, his guidance was not always in the line of safety. He led his party so far wrong in 1851 that they had to take refuge in the wilds of Kaffirland, beyond the Kei, and he himself had a price set on his head, dead or alive. He continued wandering about in mountains, and in dens and in caves of the earth, often fighting in self defence, sometimes for the kaffirs, sometimes against them, until he reached Nomansland. Once he was held at bay in the bush over against the farm "*Boschkloof*," on the western edge of the Kokstad commonage, and was reduced to the dire necessity of slaughtering and eating his dogs. This circumstance is commemorated in the name of the spruit—"*Droevig*" which, in full, was "*Droevige Toestand*," or "*Miserable Plight*." Later he and his party settled near the present *Ibisi* drift. While there an impi of kaffirs fell upon them, and almost annihilated them. Until lately, there still lived in the village of *Harding*, a Hottentot woman who was on this occasion, left for dead with 18 wounds in her body, yet she recovered. As for Pommer himself, he had almost a charmed life and wounds in every limb. All this was late in the fifties, before Kok's advent to Nomansland. Pommer allied himself with Kok, and for a time tried to force himself gracefully to take a subordinate place. He led a commando in the little war with Tiba, on the banks of the Umzimkulu in 1858. He took up his residence in *Riet Vley*, under the ægis of Kok, and lost no opportunity of gaining fresh influence among the kaffir tribes. That influence was just ripening into danger for *Kok* in the early seventies. Unprepossessing though he was, he married perhaps the most attractive girl in the country, the daughter of a worthy man, Ulbrecht, the father of a large family of stalwart worthy sons. That Pommer hatched treason there is, I think, no doubt. Events showed that he imbued his brothers-in-law with his own spirit of insubordination. Pommer was an anarchist, out-and-out. He might have said, with a certain Irishman, who, when he was asked, on landing in America, what party he would vote for said, he did not know, but, "in any case he was agin the governmint!" Pommer was at bottom against all social order. He was a dead shot; rode a horse like a cowboy; had an iron constitution, and was absolutely without fear of God or man, beast or devil. He had much to do with the rising of 1878. He contended that as Capt. Blyth held his court in the presence of armed policemen, the Griquas should also be heard stating their grievances with arms in their hands. He took the lead of the Riet Vley party. At his instigation wagons were plundered in the Zuurberg. After the battle of Mount Currie he tried to escape, leading his party to Pondoland He had now the unique distinction, that for a second time a price was put upon his head. Donald Strachan and his men overtook Pommer, and he was shot. His body was brought to Kokstad, tied to the back of a led horse, and buried in the corner of the Government erf., beside the Kok monument. Death had ended his intrigues. Though at heart an anarchist, Pommer was not without his good qualities. He was generous, kind, sympathetic, ready to respond to any cry of distress, and especially ready to champion, with a rough chivalry, the cause of any wronged woman.

Mauritz Pretorious.—This was a very obscure individual in the little town, yet he also, in his way, made his contribution to South African history. Born in Cape Town towards the end of the eighteenth century, he remembered seeing, and could graphically describe, *General Baird's* entry into the city in 1806. The circumstance which fixed his attention, and remained most distinctly in his memory, was the march of the Highlanders. "Mal koppen met vrowens rokken!" ("Madmen in women's clothes!") While still a youth, he was leader to *Dr. Van der Kemp's* waggon from Cape Town to *Bethelsdorp*. There he received his religious training. He was one of the original grantees of the Kat River Settlement, but, like many more, sold out his allotment at the first moment that selling became possible. Thence he went to Bechuanaland, and assisted in the rough work of establishing the mission station at *Kuruman*. On his return journey, he halted at *Philipolis*, and settled down there. He claimed to be the original grantee of the farm on which *Bloemfontein* now stands, and he was the man who gave it *its* present name. He held the certificate from the local fieldcornet. I am aware that later the farm stood registered in the name of a Dutch Boer, and that Dr. Theal represents this man as the original grantee, but he is wrong. There is unanimity of opinion amongst the old Griquas that Mauritz first broke soil on the spot which became, in after years, the Republican capital. Ownership of farms in those days and in those regions rested on a somewhat uncertain tenure. About 1883, Pretorious, somewhat reluctantly, was persuaded to lend the said certificate (which I have myself seen and read) to the late Rev. James Read, of Philipton, Kat River. He intended to make some literary use of it. It got lost among Mr. Read's papers, and up till now all efforts to recover it have failed. He was a handy man, could do a little at almost anything. He worked at the Griqua parsonage, school and church from start to finish. *Mauritz* could not keep money—not a sixpence! He was equally well off earning two shillings a day, in kind, as when he received five shillings in cash. A week's wages, drawn on Saturday, were all gone by Monday; yet he did not drink, except occasionally kaffir beer. He had a supreme contempt for the Griqua Government—all its officers and doings. "Domme menschen, weet nix," he would say. ('Blockheads, they know nothing!") He had some good qualities, but his ethics were terribly defective, and his conscience somewhat elastic on all questions of *meum* and *tuum*. The old man of seventy years of age married a young woman for his third wife. One day he stood up to have his youngest child baptized, side by side with his great grandchild, bringing her first-born. Mauritz declined to select his farm in *Nomansland*, though entitled to do so. "*Kan nie grond eet nie.*" ("I can't eat ground.") After annexation however, he was in a great hurry to secure it. As soon as he got the scrap of paper from the *land board*, certifying that he was entitled to a grant of land, he hawked it about for a purchaser. *Capt. Blyth* and myself tried to persuade him not to sell, even advanced money to meet immediate wants. It was no use. Sell he would and sell he did, for, I think, something like £75. Then he and his family fared sumptuously every day, and in six months nothing was left but a lean horse, a saddle and bridle and a few rags of clothing Mauritz never worried himself about anything except food; when he had none he helped himself. When he had no tobacco, he became first silly, then excited, and then next to mad. When he was over eighty years of age he walked still with a firm step. He never had an hour's sickness, worked till the last day, and died from sheer exhaustion of vital functions.

GERT BEZUIDENHOUT.—This Griqua man was, I consider, one of the excellent of the earth, if tested by the divine standards. He was not learned in the schools, nor cultured, nor brilliant, nor clever. He was good; his ethics were sound; his heart was true; his life was clean—an upright man. I believe he was morally incapable of an ignoble, mean, or deceitful action. Judged not by the creed of men, or the world's code of honour, but by the principles of the Sermon on the Mount, this man was as near to perfection as any man I have known. A real Christian gentleman, though clothed in plain garments and covered by a dark skin. I give him a place here as one of a class who professed and called themselves Christians, and were a credit to the name. Gert was one of a large family, bearing the family name, and that, like most names, obtaining amongst the Griquas, pointed to a Dutch parentage. The name and the colour together proclaimed the old disgraceful story. The Bezuidenhout family is widely spread in South Africa. A relative of the Kokstad Bezuidenhouts held a not inconsiderable slice of the land on which Johannesburg now stands, and especially that which became the famous *City and Suburban Gold Mine*. *Gert* was brother-in-law to the late chief *Nicholas Waterboer*. He often told me of playing with the "klein blink klippjes"—"the little shining stones"—when he was a child, along the banks of the Vaal River—which "shining stones," he afterwards recognised as the diamonds which made his old haunts and hunting ground famous. Gert fought at Boom Plaats, and after the fight tended some of the wounded Boers. Gert was one of the annuitants of the "forty years' money," under the Smith Treaty. He saw the treaty signed, and heard the threats and strong language of the Governor at Bloemfontein. He saw produced at Philipolis the bag of gold sovereigns sent by Sir James Clerk to tempt the Griquas to consent to a treaty which was a transparent noose of the rope with which the new Republic was to strangle the little state. He owned and worked the farm Rooi Poort, at the foot of the Zuurberg, till strength gave way, then sold out and built a house in Kokstad, to be near the church. He held, through his wife, valuable properties in Griqualand West. He empowered a Griqua agent to sell and administer this estate, which the agent did, to his own benefit, but poor Gert never saw a brass farthing of all the proceeds. He declined to prosecute. Losing faith in his coloured agent, he next time tried the white. He became executor for a Griqua estate, valued at £750. He employed an attorney practising in Kokstad to administer it for him, with the result that the attorney got convicted of embezzlement, poor Gert had to make good the attorney's defalcations, and Gert, between the two mill-stones, had his own little estate ground to powder. Gert was a notable figure at all political "vergaderings," but would have nothing to do with the doings of the "Committee of 12." He invariably spoke, but never with bitterness. His appeal was ever to Treaties Conventions, promises. He had them all at his finger tips, but invariably exhausted the patience and time of his hearers, by useless details, before he reached his point. He reminded me of the boy who took a mile of a race to jump a low wall, and when he reached it he had no breath left. Gert was for many years the treasurer of the Griqua Church. He was not much of an accountant, but his honesty withstood all weathers. He died as he had lived, content and at peace with all the world, and glad with the hope that maketh not ashamed. Peace be to the ashes of this good man His widow was the sister and the daughter of the Chief with whom we made treaties. and she received a pauper's dole from Government till she died.

CHAPTER XVII.

For some time there was little appearance of change in the methods of government. *Edward Barker* was appointed to act for *Orpen*, who still remained at the Tsitsa. *Barker* was to assist *Adam Kok* in his clerical work. Everthing went on pretty much as before, with the one exception, that Kok ceased to have the right to alot farms and erven. Up till now, any man of colour who would undertake Burgher responsibilities and duties, could have a farm of three thousand acres in extent, and an erf in town, for the asking. He had to pay the *Field-cornet* of the Ward 7s. 6d. a day for going round, and pointing out the farms still open for allotment. When he had made his selection he received from the officer what was called a "*Request*," or certificate, which declared that A. B. was the first applicant for the farm C.; here followed the name the selector chose to give the farm, and a very rough description of its position. With this certificate in hand he could take out Title on payment of an office fee of 10s. Many were content with the certificate, which was equally good, provided that no dispute arose.

It will be seen that the annual quit rent was £2, but up till 1874 this might be paid in kind, if cash was not to be had. Any white man willing to put his dignity, if he had any, into his pocket, and apply to the Raad, might be accepted as a Burgher, under the usual conditions of military service—a very unlikely contingency, and forthwith became entitled to select his farm and erf. Very amusing are the stories of how farms were sometimes granted. It must be understood that these farms went a-begging for owners. It was said that old *Van*

Wyke, an Amsterdamer, who had settled on the farm, "*Sneezewoodfontein*," applied for farms, not only for his sons already born, but for those *in expectancy*. He urged that he was quite confident about their arrival in due time; that he had already decided on their names; that it would be a clear saving of time and trouble to make out all the titles in a bundle, and he would find the land all adjoining. "You give me the farms, Chief, and I shall find the boys." "No, no," said the Chief, "a boy must be able to bring his father a glass of water or a live coal for his pipe before he can have a farm." These juvenile attainments became the recognised qualifications for a child becoming a landed proprietor. Some white men qualified themselves for Burgher rights by marrying a Griqua wife, and some by pretending to do so, but leaving a convenient back door.

At the date of annexation the average value of land was about 3d. an acre. The farm "GLENROCK," near to Kokstad, was sold by the original grantee for cattle and blankets, of the value of about £12. The following farms were pressed upon the writer by the original grantees: Fair View ("*Leeuw Kop*"), for £40; "*Strydfontein*," by "*Hottentot Pienaar*," for £30; "*Koppies Kraal*," by a Basuto widow, for £40; "*Nairn*," by Jan Welkom, for £40; "*Bloemfontein*," near to Young's, at Glengarry, for six trek oxen, value about £4 each; "*Oliphants Hoek*," by Oosthuizen, for £32. I give these as examples. Each of these farms would measure, approximately, three thousand acres.

Many of the Griquas who owned farms made little use of them. If a Griqua happened to run out of draught oxen, his farm became practically useless to him. Dig he would not, and plough he could not. Every Griqua who had crossed the mountain, and his grown-up children, were entitled to farms. Many refused to take up their grants because they were too poor to work or stock them. Annexation placed these men in the position not of owners, but expectants of land. They had to wait the convenience of the Government and the sitting of the Land Board. Most of them were in no hurry before 16th October, in fact, could not be persuaded to select their allotments, but when they had to wait, in some cases, for years, in uncertainty and suspense, they became dissatisfied, and joined in the general outcry against Government. This seems, at first sight, somewhat hard, but when it is remembered that surveys had not been completed, that much uncertainty existed as to the extent of land available, and the amount already alienated under title, no one can blame the Government for putting a stop to the somewhat reckless distribution which had obtained. That the Government meant to act in good faith, to satisfy every just claim, to divide the land amongst the people whose claims remained unsatisfied, is, I think, absolutely certain. That Government reserved none of the land originally

JAN BERGOVER, Treasurer to the Griqua Government.

Kokstad from the Stony Kopje in 1878, looking South. F.A.M.P. Camp in the foreground.

intended by *Adam Kok*, for distribution among the Griquas, with one or two exceptions, is, I think, equally certain. The question of *Kaffir Locations*, a burning one among the Griquas, will be treated hereafter.

The Griquas could see no need for this waiting for surveys, Land Commission, etc. Because they could not have their grants at once, they fumed and fretted, sat for days in meetings, got up memorials, sent deputations, issued protests, etc. They even talked of sending a deputation to England. "Let us send and talk with the old lady." They beat the empty air, and left the land untilled. Stories were set in circulation to the effect that "they would be heavily taxed. Every head of stock, even to fowls, pigs, goats, dogs, cats, and every pane of glass would have to pay rates. They would never be able to pay the taxes, and the end would be they would be turned into locations." They, foolishly, believed anything and everything to the discredit of the Government. It was not to the interest of those who wanted to buy as much land as possible, and as cheaply as possible, to contradict these stories which mysteriously came into circulation. It helped little that myself, and others, made our tongues sore, and our throats hoarse, shouting "*Don't sell your land*," or to assure the people that these stories were not true. The more we preached thus the more determined the infatuated people seemed to do the opposite.

Doubtless, one explanation of this sudden and general mania for farm-selling may be found in the fact that they had, for years, been deprived of their accustomed pleasure of handling money. Now, when money was obtainable, for land, they could not be persuaded to resist the temptation of merely handling the cash.

To add to the dissatisfaction and suspicion, *Mr. Orpen* commissioned *Mr. E. Barker* to proceed to take a *Census* of the country souls, cattle, stock of all kinds, and including wagons, carts, fruit trees, etc. This was as fuel to the flame. Kokstad became a land market. Buyers came from all quarters. The foolish people sold titled farms, town erven, and even the right or chance of obtaining these They believed, or pretended to believe, that even after the Land Board had heard their claims these claims would not receive recognition ; but if they sold to a white man, he would be a *persona grata* with Government, and get what it would be impossible for them to secure. They argued thus : "Better get something now than wait on and, perhaps, get nothing at all." So these claimants sold their rights, and, afterwards, gnashed their teeth at their consummate folly, when they saw the beautiful farms for which they had to pass transfer. No reasoning would convince these men that they had not been injured.

This ceaseless flow of money into the country, in which, a few years ago, there had been none, brought, very soon, facilities for spending it. Durban firms ran up stores of wood and iron, and stocked them well, and did a roaring trade. Pedlars, with cheap jewellery, "*Simouses*," with all kinds of portable goods, and in all kinds of conveyances, crowded into the country. No such mania for land selling has been witnessed in South Africa since the days of the Trek Boers. Of course, many of the owners of farms were not fitted to be landed proprietors, except under stringent restrictions as to sale. "Beggars mounted run their horses to death" Fully one-half of the six hundred Griqua farms passed out of the possession of the people by the end of the third year after annexation. Many thousands of acres of excellent agricultural and grazing lands were sold for 6d. an acre, even after annexation had given fixity of tenure and security of title. Annexation, to the European, gave added value to the land while to the Griquas, because of the imaginary burdens it became almost worthless. Hence the mad race after the land dealer. There were, doubtless, burghers who took advantage of the ignorance, and prejudice, and weakness of the people, and wheedled them into selling; but perhaps as many sellers worried the buyers to buy. The Griqua, as a general rule, if he once got the "*verkoop gedachte*," or, as we would say, the selling fever, he gave nobody rest until he found a purchaser. He asked three times as much as he expected to get; the dealer offered, perhaps, one-third of what he was prepared to give. Then the haggling began, and continued, until buyer and seller came to terms, each moving in an opposite direction. If anything could have been more deplorable than this reckless selling of valuable property, for next to nothing, it was the mad methods of spending the proceeds. Some there were who drank out the best part of the purchase money. With them the whole transaction, bargaining, selling, spending, was only a matter of a few days. Occasionally, one would see a Griqua man at the billiard or card table The windows were open to the street. "Certain lewd fellows of the baser sort" had him on their hook. The next we heard was that A.B. had sold his farm, and that very little of the price obtained was more than a few hours in his pocket. Here is what I saw one day in 1875 or '76. Hans —— has sold his farm. His pocket is jingling with gold sovereigns. It has been a rare experience with Hans for a long time. One hundred or one hundred and twenty pounds!! Why, it would never go lone. He is now no more "*Somaar een mensch*"—an ordinary mortal He holds his head high, walks with a lofty, stately tread. *Oom Hendrik*, *Neef Cootje*, and *Tanta Maria* have each borrowed something from him, without giving any kind of security, to be repaid when their turns of luck came round, meantime to bear interest at the rate of "*een shilling op de pond in de maand*"—sixty per cent. per annum, the usual rate *promised* between Griqua and Griqua, but never to my knowledge paid. And he has bought a good deal at the winkle, which he could very well have done without. He has, in some mysterious way, got something stronger than Kafir beer, and a wandering pedlar has him now in hand. "Yes, why should not *his* wife have a gold watch and a gold chain, as the white ladies have?" He will buy one, and take home as a present to *Martha*. The pedlar flatters, coaxes, cozens him, and he buys and pays a long price for a showy, worthless article He sits down on a stone to wind up the watch, inserts the key, twists it, first one way, then another, backwards and forwards, and round about, till the delicate mechanism is ground to powder. As I watched him he said, "This thing won't go, sir; what is the matter?" He would present it to his wife, when he got home, for a peace offering to a hungry, heart-broken woman, whose home had been sold over her head for a mess of pottage, and who, as likely as not, would become cook, or washer woman on the estate, and in the house where her children had been born, and where she had been mistress.

To a stranger it almost transcends belief, the childish folly with which even good men among the Griquas who abjured strong drink, gambling and such like, spent the cash obtained by the sale of the farm or erf.

In many instances when the Griquas had sold out and got the cash their creditors of long standing turned up as thickly as weeds after a summer rain. These claims had not been mentioned between them for years, so that on both sides they had come to be regarded as "written off." Hans, however, could not resist the temptation to revive and present the ancient account when he saw Piet rolling in money and he penniless. And so these old creditors presented their accounts, with a polite reminder that it was now "*English time*." A few of these old debts, and especially if Griqua rate of interest was added on, left the poor fellow with barely sufficient to replenish his scanty wardrobe or bring home a peace offering to his wife.

There were a few who, protesting against the *folly* of *selling*, tried to exhibit, by way of contrast, their superior *wisdom* by *borrowing*. It generally came to the same issue, only a little delayed, for it was the rarest event for a Griqua to redeem a bond. Landed proprietors who do not think "*one shilling a month for every pound borrowed*" an exhorbitant rate of interest, and who are willing to take up capital on these terms and hypothecate their land, are not likely to be very long in finding capitalists ready and eager to do business. If "*Oom Jan*" wanted to outstrip his neighbour in ostentatious display, and in the hospitable entertainment of half the country side, at the approaching wedding of his daughter or son, well it was quite an easy matter to borrow £50 or so. "Why, old Isaac "will let me have the money at half our interest. Aye, *at six-"pence on a pound for a month!*" That is nothing! And then "we can have a beautiful silk dress, veil and wreath, parasol "and gloves for the bride. We can have a bag of coffee and "a box of tea, and a few bags of sugar; we can hire horses and "carts and drive the wedding party to and from the Church, "and have a good time, and be like the white people for once "in our lives. Why not?" And so the deeds are duly handed over to the usurer, and the borrower binds himself to repay at the end of three or six months, principal and interest, and failing that to sell the farm for so much. Meantime, bad health has come to the family, or lung-sickness has come among the stock, or a hail storm has destroyed the ripening crop of wheat, and the source from which relief was expected has failed, and the borrower is in the clutch of the lender. Interest is now added to the capital, and a new bond signed. Thus it goes on till the borrower finds his neck in the halter, gives up in despair and sells to get out of the mess

In the main the above is a transcript of the secret history of scores of landsales in Griqualand East Expensive and extravagant weddings put the first nail in the coffin of many a goodly Griqua estate. If the minister, or indeed anyone, pointed out the folly and madness of it all, then he would probably get credited with a secret desire the keep down the coloured man from an improved social position.

A GRIQUA LAMENT.

Bring me here that old Dutch banjo. Methinks I hear one of the old Griqua men giving vent to a kind of easy-going, jocose, repentance over his folly in selling his farm, and his still greater folly in the spending of the money. I want to accompany him. His words awaken some old and painful memories. Now then, play up:

Mij plaats is verkoop, de geld is gedaan,
De kos is al op met de laatste maan
De vrouw zit en huil, haar oogen is rood,
De kindern kla in bitteren nood.

Mij kop was op hol, door maakers, gebracht.
De goed uit de winkel, was boven mij magt.
Die schuld te betaal, de schaap moet ik scheer,
Dan gaan illa weg, illa keer niet weer.

't Dobblen en't drinken krappen mij kaal,
Niet meer, staat er perd of os in de kraal.
'T's waar ik was dom, ik voel nu berouw,
Engelsman toch is Griqua te gaauw.

Zuur is de appel ik moet nu door bijt,
Niets zal't mij helpen mijn jammer en spijt.
Van alls is ik kwijt, van huis en van haard,
'K weet nie al is ik een dubbeltje waard.

Perhaps the saddest part of this miserable business lay in this, that these people would not realise that, in selling their farms, they parted with the right to influence the Government in administering the affairs of the country. For instance—

The *Griqua law* prohibited the sale of or even the importation of *Strong Drink*. The spirit and the purpose of the prohibition was occasionally violated and evaded, by the Chief himself, when he sent over the border for a private supply. Still there was the *law*. On one occasion, while the people were still living in the old Laager, the violation of the law by a trader, not only brought on him penalties, but the confiscation of the contrabrand article. *Lodowijk Kok* was magistrate at the time. He had found out that a cask of Natal rum had been secretly imported, and lay concealed among the stuff in the shop loft. He had it rolled out of the store, the head driven in, and left the contents to run down the gutter—the very best place for it.

The law, notwithstanding the occasional breaches, was the salvation of the tribe, and they all knew it. When annexation took place one of the strongest objections raised was that "*Colonial rule will bring Colonial brandy and canteens, and that will ruin us.*" I am not aware that any written promise was ever given, but I can bear testimony that *Adam Kok* was assured by *Sir Henry Barkly*, and by *Mr. Orpen*, that "*Canteens would not be sanctioned* in the Griqua country." Possibly this promise was given when John Bull was in his very best of humour—quite prepared to promise anything. Had the Griquas held their lands by communal title, as in the case of the Basutos, these lands would have been inalienable, and the country would have remained Griqua country. Had the majority of the people retained possession of their lands and erven, they and their friends could have insisted on Government keeping its promise. But when European farm-owners came largely to outnumber Griqua owners, the country ceased to be Griqua country, in the sense in which the Governor had made the promise. The wishes of the new owners and occupiers had to be considered. They claimed to stand in the shoes of the original grantees. They demanded hotels and canteens as a necessity of civilization, and got them. The Griqua could not see the fine distinction, and here was another grievance. The Griqua argued, and with some show of reason, "You bought this farm under the Griqua prohibitory "law. If power to influence the policy of Government went "with the land, from me to you, you simply stand in my "place, and are bound, in good faith, to support the prohibi-"tion." But the new owner could not see it, or did not want to.

Or take a somewhat similar case. The promise was, that for some time, at least, they would continue to be governed *under Griqua law.* Griqua law was more prescriptive and traditional than statutory and written. The evidence led as to a particular law or custom was often very contradictory, notably so in reference to the *Laws of Inheritance* The impartial administration of law and justice was a new thing. Once the Griquas began to see that this impartiality existed, they gained confidence. It greatly reconciled the honest and more respectable men among them to the new regime. But it evoked *litigation* which, under the old Government, would never have been thought of. Executors who had never administered estates were called on by heirs, to render account, and to divide the ancient inheritance If the one side took a stand on equity, or on the law of the Colony, the other might plead that English or Colonial law was not in force. If appeal was made to Griqua law, then proof had to be led as to what Griqua law was, and the confusion became worse confounded. When executors, either under the one law or the other, had to disgorge, and pay up, they did not like it, and inveighed against the new magistrates as being hard on them. The heirs, on the other hand, who had now got back their own, were equally loud in praise of English fair play. These inheritance and estate cases cropped up, and kept the little town in a state of ferment during the years '75 and '76, and many were the grotesque situations created. Reports of the work done in the courts in those days would be entertaining reading. Had the Griquas retained possession of the country, the administration of Griqua law, with all its vagaries, might have become, approximately, possible, but when the European owners became the majority, and refused to have their case tried under Griqua law, the difficulties became almost unsurmountable.

CHAPTER XVIII.

Adam Kok now (1874) withdrew from public business. *Mr. Orpen* remained at Tsitsa. Mr. *Barker*, had, at first, not even the authority of a J.P. He administered in Kok's name, and consulted him in every matter, except where he received instructions from Orpen. The *Volksraad* met shortly after the Governor had left, and discussed the situation with their accustomed volubility, but with little outcome. The burden of their song, as may be seen from the Dutch ditty, might be put thus: "The Chief gets £1,000 per annum, the Councillors £36 per annum each. What do we get? *Nix, nix, nix!*" "Nothing! Do you hear?—nothing!" Here the shoe pinched. At length, it was decided to send a *Deputation* to Capetown to urge on the Government to make a *Retrocession* of the country. I believe that the idea was to get things back to the position before October, '74, then let them talk, confer, haggle, and bargain with a Governor's agent, and have the terms embodied in a *Treaty*, as became the dignity of an independent nation. Mr. D. Strachan and Mr. C. Brisley were deputed to go. Both had enjoyed Burgher rights. They had had almost a land monopoly, and had bought freely before annexation. Annexation meant, to them, immediate wealth. Retrocession would defer that wealth by deferring the certain rise in the value of land. The folly of expecting these two men to be enthusiastic advocates of Retrocession was plain to everyone. It is, indeed, doubtful if any of the parties concerned seriously meant what they said, when they shouted for "*De land terug*"*!* "*De land terug*"*!*—"Retrocession! Retrocession!"

The deputation saw *Mr. Brownlee*, and returned bringing a "*Despatch*" with them. The Chief called a meeting on the Market Square. It was one of the largest which had been held, and the letter was read. To ordinary mortals, like myself, there appeared not one word to justify the construction which was put upon it—that the annexation had been reversed, and "*De land is terug.*" Certain minor concessions had been made. A *Resident Magistrate* was to be sent, and with him, Adam Kok was to exercise *co-ordinate jurisdiction*. The people returned from that meeting in a high state of jubilation, shouting "DE LAND IS TERUG." Fireworks, in the evening, increased the excitement. In a few days they began to realise that there was to be no retrocession. I do not think the *Volksraad* ever met after that. The agitation began again, and the *Committee of Twelve* was now called into existence. When, or by whom, it was appointed, nobody seems to know. It was largely the creation of *Adam Smith*, who remained its moving spirit, chairman, and scribe. It was to be the mouthpiece of the people to the Government. It met monthly, and got through a pretty considerable amount of talk, and prepared memorials, petitions, etc., all quite harmless, very ambiguous, and generally bristling with what logicians call "*begging the question.*" As I have said elsewhere, this Committee was the safety valve of the political machine.

Meantime, *Mr. Orpen* took umbrage at the Commissioners and at *Kok*, and his Raad. He paid a visit to Kokstad, and ransacked the Griqua archives, which he had sealed up on the 16th October. Finding evidence of what he chose to regard as criminality, on the part of Kok and his officials, and failing to persuade *Mr. Brownlee* to a course of action, which *Mr. Brownlee* considered bad taste, and in bad faith, he set off to Cape town, if possible to force the Secretary's hand. High words followed between them. Orpen resigned, and raised an agitation against *Kok*, *Strachan*, *Brisley*, and *Brownlee*, first in the press, and thereafter from his new seat in Parliament. Thereafter, Mr. J. M. Orpen disappears from the scene.

CHAPTER XIX.

T. A. Cumming, Esq., arrived in Kokstad on 25th March, 1875. He was commissioned to exercise a *dual* jurisdiction along with *A. Kok*, who could have made things very uncomfortable for him, had he been built that way. He was not cantankerous, and, besides, he was glad to be relieved of the cares of office. Cumming soon found out that he could do pretty much as he liked. He was, perhaps, the most suitable man Government could have sent in the, then, anomalous position of affairs He was not a young man, he knew Dutch, knew the kind of people he had to deal with, their ways of thinking, their good and bad qualities, especially he knew exactly where the tender corns were. He received them courteously when they came to ventilate a grievance, cracked a joke, handed round his snuff-box, had a good, long, free-and-easy talk, with the result that the men who had come protesting against all kinds of things went away somewhat ashamed at their own folly and shortsightedness. He beat no drum, hoisted no flag, uttered no threats, had no police, made no changes He quietly smiled at the harmless vapouring of the *Committee of Twelve* "Let them talk, it's only talk; they don't mean anything," he said, and he was quite right.

About this time, the question was raised, "Can we not have some *Regulations* as to *trespass*, the kraaling of cattle, and impounding of stray stock in the town?" A public meeting of erfholders was called At that meeting the Griquas learned, for the first time, *that the Chief had, from the start, contemplated the establishment of a* MUNICIPALITY, *and that their titles committed them to it.* The Griquas have always displayed a marked hostility to the idea of Municipal Government. This is in singular contrast to their equally uniform and strong contention for independence, "*Zelfstandigheid.*" Regulations were now drawn up, few and simple, and passed by the vote of the erfholders. They accepted the principle of Home Rule, or Civic Government, and acted on it. Their subsequent action in opposing the establishment of a *Municipality* in the nineties, and their almost uniform opposition since then, to all measures for the improvement of the town, can only be accounted for by the fixed aversion of nearly all native and coloured citizens to *direct* taxation, and the ignorance which blinds them to the fact that every public improvement increases the value of the public estate, raises the standard of civilisation, and increases the facilities for comfort and enjoyment. They are not lacking in obedience to the divine command, "be fruitful and multiply," but they, conveniently, forget that the same authority commands them "to replenish the earth and subdue it."

From 1871 up to the beginning of 1874 each erfholder buried his dead in his own erf. The Government had not selected a place of burial. I declined to do so, believing it to belong more to the functions of the State than to the Church. I refused to attend any funeral in a private erf, after a certain date. Then the Chief and his Council selected the spot now used as Town Cemeteries. It was intended to be *for all classes, creeds, and colours*, and was so used for some time. A Griqua girl, who had been confirmed in the *Church of England*, died. Mr. Dixon, as representing that church, applied for a separate piece of ground, to become a denominational cemetery. The Chief said, "If it had been a white person, I could have "understood your objection to mingling the ashes of the dead, "on the score of colour, but on the score of creed, I cannot "understand it. However, if you will have it so, select a "separate place on the same ridge, and bury the girl."

In June, 1875, Colonel, then Mr. Griffith, of Basutoland, and S. Probart, Esq., M.L.A., and Mr. Cumming were appointed a *Commission*, to make careful inquiry into the bona-fides of all land transactions by the Griqua Government, and to investigate as to the claims of those who had not yet received their grants of land, and to report. These three gentlemen sat in the house in the Main street already described. *Mr. Barker* was elected Secretary. They applied themselves daily with diligence to the discharge of this difficult task. Each burgher personally appeared and produced his title, if he had any. It was then compared with the duplicate in the Government book. If a burgher held a certificate or a "*request*," that, also, was handed in, and careful inquiry made as to the validity of the grant, or the justice of the claim founded on it. In doubtful cases the Chief was consulted. There were scores of applicants for farms and erven, who would never have dreamed of setting up such claims under Griqua rule. The annexation had emphasised the idea of *equality*. Jack was now as good as his master, provided he had the dark colour; indeed, he was inclined to think he was a good deal better. The more respectable portion of the Griquas were amazed and amused at the temerity of some of the applicants. Every bushman boy who, as groom or wagon driver, had crossed the mountain with them, considered that he was entitled to a "plaats." and fumed and fretted when his claims were disregarded.

The work of this Commission was unduly hurried by the following circumstances: *Earl Carnarvon*, Imperial Colonial Secretary, had sent the late *Mr. Froude* as his emissary, to quietly force on the Colony cut-and-dried schemes of *Confederation*. The Cape Cabinet resented this interference with the independence of the Colony, under the new constitution, and summoned Parliament. Probart was ambitious of office, and could not brook being absent from so important a sitting; hence the haste, so that he might be in time.

While the Commission sat, the *Committee of Twelve* had several interviews with it The Griquas so utterly wearied them with the length and discursiveness of their speeches, that it all looked like searching for a needle in a haystack. These meetings raised a considerable amount of excitement in the little town. Mr. Probart was the clown of the party. He instinctively saw things from the humorous side. Nearly every case which came up for investigation had its ludicrous features. These Probart recorded by pen and pencil. Some of his sketches will be found in the *Cape Monthly* for February, 1876. The report of this Commission formed the *basis of Government action in all future dealings with allotted farms and erven.* It acted on the following principles:—

(1) That the land claims of all bona-fide title-holders were to be first provided for.
(2) Next to them came the claims founded on Certificates.
(3) That the aggregate acreage of Locations, for the use of Kaffir and Basuto tribes, should be approximately maintained.
(4) That the balance of land remain for distribution among (*a*) landless burghers who trekked over the mountain; (*b*) their adult sons; (*c*) residents with the Griquas who had done public service.

All these principles of land distribution received the assent of the Griquas, except the third, which became and has remained the great bone of contention between them and the Government, almost until this day. The controversy might be put in a nutshell, thus:—

Griquas: "We claim that all the land in the Basuto and Kaffir locations ought to be reserved for distribution amongst us and our children. Is it not Griqualand?"

Government: "We simply confirm and continue occupation, of the same aggregate of location lands as was *made by the Griqua Chief and his Government.* The Griqua Government had its representative *Volksraad*, which, by its silence, consented to the alienation of the locations, and drew from these its chief revenue."

Thus things moved on until the end of 1875. Mr. Cumming, by his quiet, conciliatory ways, was gradually killing opposition and disloyalty. The Griquas were eagerly awaiting the report of the Commission. The *Committee of Twelve* were meeting and talking every month, and then going home more contented and reconciled with the inevitable. Month by month the political ginger beer bottle got brisk, went off with its accustomed fiz, and then all was comparatively quiet again.

CHAPTER XX.

Adam Kok died on the 30th December, 1875. The event occurred in this wise: The Chief was living at Leuw-Kop (now Fair View). From this place he started on the morning of that day, in the company of *Jan Jood* and his family. They were all proceeding to keep the new year at Umzimkulu. The Chief drove in a buggy, and along with him his wife's grand-children. They rested, and had luncheon at "*Stafford's*," who treated the party with his wonted hospitality. Resuming the journey, all went well till they came to a spot which I shall try to describe, so that the traveller may easily identify it.

Coming along the old road, between Riet Vley and Umzimkulu, the traveller, after passing the junction of this road and the *Harding* road, descends to a drift. Passing from the drift up the deep cutting, if he look to the left he will see, about two hundred yards distant, the spoor of an old road, which was in use before this cutting was made The spot where this old spoor joins the present road is the exact place where Adam Kok met his death. At this spot the Chief stood up to touch with his whip a young horse leading in the team, and used the whip vigorously just as the cart wheel struck the slanting rut of the old road. The spurt of the horse, the jerk and swing of the vehicle, threw him off his balance. He fell before the wheel, which passed over his chest. He rose, placed his hand on his chest, and said, "*Ach, wat is dit nu?*" ("Oh! what is this now?" He staggered and fell, and never rose again. Wagon and cart were immediately outspanned. The dying chief was gently laid on the grass, under the wagon. He occasionally groaned, once he asked for water, but besides that uttered not a word, and expired about four o'clock, two hours after the accident. These particulars of the Chief's last moments were related to me by Jan Jood, and confirmed by his wife. They do not quite agree with Mr. Brisley's letter, but it must be remembered that Mr. Brisley was not present, and wrote his letter in great haste and agitation. Messengers were despatched to Umzimkulu, to Mr. Brisley, who had a rough coffin hurriedly constructed, and brought to the spot during the night. Early in the morning they all started back with the dead chief for Kokstad.

Early in the day a horseman brought to me the following letter:—

"Build Fontein,
"Thursday night,
"30th December, '75.

"My Dear Mr. Dower,—

"It is my sad duty to inform you that the Kaptyn met with an accident to-day, and fell from his trap, which passed over him and broke his ribs. He only survived two hours, and did not seem to have suffered much pain. He never spoke after the accident. We are having a shell coffin made for him here, and intend to start for Kokstad early in the morning, and expect to get there to morrow evening. His wish was that he should be buried in the corner of his erf, S.W., nearest opposite the erf of Adam Smith. Would you kindly at once get a proper coffin made that will be large enough to hold the shell. I think they will simply make it this shape

and the cover coffin should be about 7 feet by 2 feet 2 inches at top, and sufficiently deep. We cannot defer the funeral later than Saturday morning Do not let any expense stand in the way. Would you also see that Klein Klaas (to whom I have written instructions) make the grave sufficiently large and deep, and at the spot I have indicated. I have no time to write more,

"Yours very truly,

"G. C. BRISLEY.

"Rev. W. Dower,
"Parsonage,
"Kokstad."

Only a little time before this, with that singular presentiment of approaching death, which sometimes healthy men have, the Chief had pointed out this very spot as *the place where he would like to be buried.* It was a mournful and a busy day. Only when the workmen had completed their task, had we leisure to sit down and think what it all meant.

As the sun was sinking behind the western hills, the procession of wagons, carts, and horsemen entered the town, while the Griqua church bell tolled its melancholy dirge, and the members of the Chief's household wept and wailed in an agony of grief. Meantime, horsemen and Kaffir runners, fleet of foot, had conveyed the news to almost every corner of the land. During the night, loaded carts and wagons, men on horseback and on foot, continued to arrive. All New Year festivities were suspended. For obvious reasons, the funeral was fixed for an early hour—nine o'clock. By that time a very large number of burghers had collected. Many of them had been roused from sleep, had hastily saddled up, and ridden distances of twenty and thirty miles in the dark. The people ranged themselves in a semi-circle round the front of the "*palace.*" The coffin was brought out and laid on trestles. Some confusion arose from the absence of a responsible head. The relatives were all dazed and hesitant, wishing to do the right thing, but fearing they might do the wrong. There was no undertaker, no master of ceremonies. *Mr. Brisley*, with his wonted energy, took matters in hand, and everyone obeyed him promptly. I walked at the head of the procession. *Eta Kok*, *Adam Muis*, *Bergover*, *Cumming*, *Brisley*, *Barker*, acted as pall-bearers, while the Kok family and the women of the household took the place of chief mourners The service at the grave was brief and simple. Any attempt at prolonged speech would have let loose the fountains of grief, and would have produced a scene of weeping and lamentation. After the women folk had retired, old *Adam Eta*, the cousin of the deceased, the man who had for many years always acted as *Provisional Kaptyn*, as he stood looking into the grave, addressed the people in somewhat broken language, as follows, speaking in Dutch :—

"Friends and Fellow-Burghers,—We have made a sad "beginning to this new year. We have laid in this grave a "man you all knew and loved. He is the last of his race. "After him, there will be no coloured king or chief in Colonial "South Africa. Of Kaffir tribes, there may still be chiefs ; of "coloured chiefs he is the last Take a good look into that "grave. You will never look into the grave of another chief "of our race Do you realise that our nationality lies buried "there ? The deceased was the friend of you all. Did you "ever hear of *Adam Kok* making an enemy ? Political enemies "he had, unfortunately, more than his share ; private enemies "he had none. He had his faults—we all have ; but you will "all bear me out, he was generous to a fault—too indulgent, "and gentle, and yielding, for a chief. There lie the remains "of the one South African chief who never lifted arms nor "fired a shot at a British soldier, though sometimes provoked "beyond human endurance. There is not a single man here "who has not received favours at his hand. If you are ever "tempted to forget him, turn to the titles of your properties, "and see there his familiar sign manual I have yielded to "the temptation to add this much to what the minister has "said, because I am his near relative, and he honoured me "with his confidence, and occasionally delegated to me his "authority. There are many who will arrive here too late in "the day to be with us at his interment. Let us set guards, "and leave the grave open till sun-down, so that these friends "from afar may have the melancholy satisfaction of seeing all "that is fit to be seen of the Chief they loved so well. Let all "questions of politics rest. Let us go home to mourn in secret "and in silence, and prepare for the funeral services to-"morrow."

These words, more truthful than merely eulogistic, were uttered with deep emotion. Sometimes the speaker could proceed only with great difficulty. The whole scene was tragic and pathetic, and will live with me while memory lasts.

People continued to arrive all day, and some affecting scenes were witnessed at the grave. At sundown it was filled up and temporarily bricked over. On the following day I preached funeral sermons inside the roofless walls of the new church, in the blazing sun, to a very large concourse of people.

Here let me lay a chaplet on the old man's grave.

A FUNERAL DIRGE.

O Burghers kind! seek all a find,
Some seemly token of our woe;
The church bell toll, the salt tear roll,
The great man of our race lies low.

Ah, well we may, this New Year's Day,
The bitter herbs of sorrow eat;
Stay, wonted play, let's all to pray,
The very lambs in pity bleat.

The old year's sped, the old chief's dead,
Who, who, can fitly fill his place?
Lay him to rest where he thought best,
This last man of a chieftain race.

O cruel Fate! that will not wait,
The sorrowing crowds which love calls in,
To drop a tear around his bier,
Ere death's sharp teeth their work begin.

* * *

Twenty five Years' Thereafter.

What shapeless heap stands by the street,
Rugged and bare, and crumbling down?
The old Chief's grave?—'twas he who gave
The site, the charge to build the town.

Some seemly mark in hall or park,
Oh, surely, surely, well might be,
To him who founds a town that sounds
His name each day by land or sea.

Before we finally take leave of Adam Kok, let me give some reminiscences of the man as I found him, and came to know him, and it may not be amiss to note at how many points he touched upon our South African history, and at the singularly unique place he occupied in our crudescent colonial civilisation:—

Fifty years ago the name of this chief was known to most colonists, and it was, by no means, unfamiliar to the Government officials at Capetown, or to the men who directed South African affairs from the Colonial Office in London. Fifty years ago this name was also familiar enough to the friends of South African Missions, and the readers of missionary literature. To-day the name would be forgotten but for the thriving and important township which the owner thereof formed, and which the people called by his name. He was a short, stout, pock-marked man. He was not good-looking, but he was shrewd, intelligent, kindly, and hospitable. For a man who had read little, and had never been out of the country, so that he might learn from sight what he did not learn from books, he had really a wonderful knowledge of the world and its affairs.

When I joined the Griquas, in 1869, the work to be done seemed overwhelming. The Chief was, after a time, most eager and willing to help in every way possible. There was neither township nor church, school, nor dwelling-house, except of the most ramshackle and temporary character. The place of meeting had neither floor nor ceiling, door nor window, pulpit nor pew. Everything had to be started from the very foundation

At first Adam Kok was very suspicious of me, as he was of all white men, until he knew and trusted them. His suspicion bred caution, and his caution tried my patience He would wait and watch to find out what sort of fellow I was. He had crossed lances with missionaries before; he did not wish to do it again. He knew they are not all angels, and that some had more grace than gumption. This is not intended to reflect on the good man who had preceded me in Kok's old country - Rev. W. B. Philip—whose name was held in honour, and who was one of the saintliest and wisest of men. I knew that Kok was watching me, and I walked with all due circumspection. After a time I secured his confidence, and then had no difficulty in gaining his assent to my somewhat ambitious plans. For though the Church and the State were supposed to be quite separate and independent, yet, in point of fact, there never was a Church in closer alliance with the State than the Griqua Church at that time. Adam Kok was a member of its finance committee, and his word had other than its logical claims to consideration.

It was to me a trying discipline to feel pledged to inviolable theories, freshly imported from Scotland, as to the Headship of Christ, the Independence of the Church, the Sphere of the Chief Magistrate in matters ecclesiastical, and then to find that, either I must let these theories lie in abeyance or let the work of the mission stand still.

Adam Kok and his Councillors were "kittle cattle," but they were at heart not bad fellows. They required to be stroked the right way. and plenty of stroking; they required to be thoroughly convinced that you meant work and service, not merely self-seeking. Adam Kok had often to hear words from me that made his ears tingle, but he recognised that there was sincerity, fidelity, and affection at the back of the words and he listened patiently. I, on the other hand had to pocket many a little indignity, and bear all things for the Gospel's sake. Thus we rubbed against each other's angularities, and by-and-by we came right. My policy was, to get my own way by making them to believe that they were getting theirs—leading them, but keeping the string invisible. I could then get the old man to do almost anything I asked. I took good care to ask only for what was manifestly necessary and reasonable.

When the site of the new township was finally fixed on, and the survey completed, he took the liveliest interest in the erection of Mission-house, School and Church. To see a whole set of buildings, with enclosures, out-houses, gardens, gates, trees, and irrigation all planned and laid down on paper before a sod was turned, appealed to his practical mind, and completely won his confidence and co-operation. He would go to the stone quarry and the brickfield, the water furrow and the foundation trenches, asking hosts of questions. Like Josiah of old, he "made a proclamation" through East Griqualand "to bring in the collection," and "cast it into the chest." This could not literally be done, for one man brought an ox, another a load of sawn timber, a third a thousand bricks, etc. As the work proceeded, he seemed to renew his youth. We became the best of friends, and worked together very harmoniously. At first we worked with a Building Committee, which, it being large and unwieldy, was like swimming with shoes of lead. The members dropped off one by one until only Adam Kok was left, and he ceased to confer.

He spent many hours in my house. His chief delight was to see the Illustrated Magazines and hear descriptions of European life and scenes.

For such a man—simple, confiding, imitative—who had learned in his early life to look on the white man as the model to be copied, his legs had been too frequently beneath the gubernatorial mahogany. He had been too often "treated" in the tents of British generals. He had come to associate dignity, authority, power, with brandy and soda. If he took too much his consolation and defence was, "De wite menschen maken zoo" (the white men do so). Alas! too quickly do men thus run into the snares of satan! But here I am in danger of speaking evil of dignities.

This coloured man occupied a position altogether unique and anomalous. He had the absolute disposal, not in tribal, but individual title, of a country roughly-speaking 5,000 square miles in extent, and containing some of the best pastoral and agricultural lands of the Colony—a place of fruitful valleys, and of broad rivers and streams, the very birthplace of waters. He actually begged of people, white and coloured, to accept of farms. Anyone could have a 3,000 acre farm for the asking, on payment of a very nominal quitrent, and doing very easy burgher duty.

One of my lads, now the minister of a Church at Queenstown, when a little chap, was one day engaging the interest of the chief, when the following conversation took place:—"Well, my boy, would you like a 'plaats'?" (a farm). "Yes, Cap'in, I would like a place in heaven." "Ah, my boy, I cannot give you a place there, for I am not sure of one for myself."

On gala days the chief was impressive in his get-up. He allowed himself to be persuaded to appear in a general's uniform. He drew a line, however, at the cocked hat—"ugly thing," he said. The result was that at one end of royalty were the

Shop at Mount Currie in 1870.

Shop in Kokstad, 1901,
Harvey, Greenacre & Co.

Kokstad, Main Street, 1901.

odorous and unsightly "veldschoenen," at the other a greasy, battered billycock hat, and in between, blue and purple, scarlet tassels and gold lace, and Brummagen jewellery to serve as insignia of office. "He bore his honours as an ass bears gold, to groan and sweat under the business." More than once I rode beside him thus got up, and at the head of his burgher army. I suppose I filled the position of pontifex maximus of the realm!

In 1874, Sir Henry Barkly annexed the country, and swallowed the little kingdom, king, lords, commons and all—pensioned them all off—save and except the pontifex maximus. Pensions are supposed to be bad for ministers, especially when they are still young and strong.

Adam Kok pulled a wry face at the loss of the prestige of royalty, but he rather enjoyed signing his receipts for £1,000 a year. He did not enjoy his pension long nor did he live to see the church completed

He was long the bulwark of our northern border, standing sentinel between the Colony and the Matabele hordes. These had a wholesome fear of Griqua guns and marksmen. His people were the only tribe beyond the border to whom the Government considered it safe to sell fire-arms and ammunition. I can find no record of their abusing the privilege. When, by the presence of the Boers on the plains between the Orange and Vaal Rivers, our northern border became sufficiently protected, we stood aside, in spite of treaty obligations and allowed our own renegade subjects to swallow the little State which had stood for us in the breach so long and so well. Adam Kok had come in contact, during his life, with nearly every man of note in our South African official circles. He made treaties with Napier, Maitland, and Harry Smith, personally transacted business with Governors Grey, Woodhouse, and Barkly, resisted the attempted encroachments of Sir George Clerk, and paid homage to the Queen's son, Prince Alfred. Kok headed his Burghers, and fought with Harry Smith at Boomplaats, and was associated with Cathcart in his disastrous escapade in Basutoland. Saul Solomon was his political agent and adviser. No man of colour has left so deep and enduring a mark on the history and nomenclature of South Africa. Had Adam Kok chosen to stretch a point, and make a declaration regarding the original ownership of the Campbell Lands, such as the Orange Free State Government so eagerly desired, that declaration would probably have been the little weight to turn the scales when they hung evenly balanced, and change the whole drift of our South African history. Let anyone refer to the voluminous evidence collected by the Commissions of Enquiry *re* the Diamond Fields and he will meet references to Kok and his doings and those of his little State, on every page. He was the first, and so far as known to me, the only African chief to attempt the somewhat perilous experiment of substituting *individual* for communal titles to land. I know of no other chief who ever tried to substitute statue for prescriptive and traditional law. Has any other native chief ever dreamed of cutting off the right hand of arbitrary and autocratic power and voluntarily submitting to the limitations of a written constitution and the restraints of a popular Representative Assembly? He and his people accomplished the task of crossing in wheeled conveyances, the crest of the terrible Drakensberg never attempted before, nor, indeed, since. They pioneered the new country, redeemed it from the dominion of wild beasts, proved its suitability for pastoral and agricultural pursuits, and, in spite of all their many shortcomings, left an imperishable name in one of the finest districts of the Cape Colony. Peace be to the ashes of the old Griqua chief, as they lie mouldering beneath that hideous cairn of bricks, dignified by the name of "monument"! His memory deserved better treatment than it has received.

CHAPTER XXI.

While the funeral service was proceeding on Sunday, January 2nd there drove into Kokstad a mule wagon conveying two *Commissioners* from the President of the Orange Free State. They brought despatches containing a series o questions to be put to Adam Kok. These questions had reference to the original positions of certain beacons which marked the old boundary between Kok and Waterboer, at the time when the Orange Free State bought out the residuary rights of the Griqua Government, in 1861. Still more important were the questions as to the extent of Cornelius Kok's rights to the Campbell lands and Adam Kok's heirship of his estate.

At a combined meeting of the two Raads, hurriedly convened on Monday morning, it was decided, notwithstanding the fact of annexation, to proceed to the election of a *pro tem.* Successor to the deceased chief, and that he should be empowered to receive the Commissioners officially, and hear the mysterious contents of the sealed letters. As I have said elsewhere, the choice fell on a nonentity, *Cornelius van der Westhuizen.* He was a man of no intelligence, decision, or energy, but he served the purpose of a stop-gap, figure-head, or tool. He had the privilege of antiquity, and was a blameless man, so that the Raads as good as said: "Oh, let us have him, for his silver hairs will purchase us a good opinion!" When these Commissioners met the new chief and his Raad, it was found that the seals could be broken only in the presence of a J.P., or an ordained minister. Mr. Cumming was a J.P., but to call him would be *infra dig.*, and probably he would decline to attend; so I was requested to go and testify to the breaking of the unbroken seals. I remained, by request, and heard the proceedings. I have ever had a firm persuasion that the Orange Free State authorities, believing Kok to have been hurt at the recent annexation, and assuming that having his pension assured, hoped Kok would now be more disposed than in 1871 to give evidence in support of their claims, and hence this *Second Commission.* The queries had reference chiefly to the overlapping jurisdiction of petty chiefs, all of them dead several decades, whose territorial limits and the sources of their authority they themselves, when alive, probably could not have defined. As evidence that certain of these deceased chiefs once had independent authority, and that their authority had, in some way, passed over to Kok, several *staffs of office*, more like policemen's batons than King's sceptres, were produced from mysterious places, with no small confidence and pride, but no staff of office belonging to Cornelius Kok. One chief point in the queries had reference to the original position of *David*'s *Graaf.* This spot had become a very uncertain quantity. The heap of stones, which had gone for many years for *David's Graaf*, was there all right, but the contention was that these had been removed. *David* had been a petty chief in the thirties. He went a shooting, and was shot by accident, and buried where he fell. A heap of stones served, first, to mark the grave, and, later, to become an important beacon on the line between Kok and Waterboer, not far from the confluence of the Riet and Modder rivers, places now famous in the annals of the British Army. A Dutch farmer had come into possession or occupation of the farm. He, evidently, had little regard for the provisions of the Jewish legislation about the removal of landmarks, and as little for the ethics of the Decalogue, when it came to a matter of a few square miles of land. So our Dutch friend's conscience did not severely rebuke him when he spanned in his wagon, one day, loaded up the stones of David's Graaf, and moved them a few miles farther afield, thus doubling, if not trebling, the extent of his pasturage. "Why should he not do it? Nobody wanted the land. Old David would sleep as quietly without the stones as with them, and who was to know that the new beacon did not mark the original grave?" The removal of the beacon became an open secret, but who was to make a fuss about a few miles of land? Thus matters remained until diamonds were found on the banks of the Vaal, and the question arose: "In whose territory lies the diamondiferous fields?" That, again, depended partly on the question: "Where lies David's Graaf?" Well, the stones could not speak. The actors in the tragic burial of David were all dead, except a few old men in Griqualand East. Hence the Commission of 1871 at old Mount Currie, and the comic issue of their having to whirl their thumbs and wait the convenience of his Griqua Majesty, and then get "'k weet nie" ('I don't know") for an answer. Hence, too, the tragic issue of coming a second time to find the Chief a few hours in his grave, and a bogus successor on his throne. My readers will now see the importance of this inquiry, and the reason for all this formality and mystery, sealed documents, and written questions.

The position, briefly statel, lay thus: In August, 1861, Adam Kok and his Council, in anticipation of the trek, authorised their agent to sell to the Orange Free State all unallotted land still belonging to them. The agent either carelessly, or of set purpose, introduced into the deed of sale the clause, "*Likewise that of the late Cornelius Kok.*" In so doing, he exceeded his powers. When the diamonds were discovered, the Orange Free State set up its claim, on the ground that Adam Kok was heir to Cornelius Kok; that Cornelius Kok had exercised sovereign rights over the now disputed territory, and these rights of Adam and Cornelius Kok had been bought out by the O.F.S. All this Waterboer disputed, contending that Cornelius Kok never had sovereign rights, that he died intestate and had heaps of children; that Adam Kok never was his heir; that the old lines mutually agreed on between him and Kok threw the fields clearly into his territory.

The controversy between the O.F.S. and the Governor of the Cape had been long and acrimonious. At last the Colonial Secretary had invited President Brand to confer with him in ngland with a view to settlement. The O.F.S Government expected now to obtain evidence to strengthen their case.

The new Chief had been one of the *signatories* to the Power of Attorney under which the sale to the O.F S. had been completed, and, moreover, was *one of the few living witnesses of the burial of David*, the place of whose grave was in dispute.

Hours were now occupied in vain effort to gain fresh evidence of Cornelius Kok's ownership of the disputed territory, and the late Adam Kok's inheritance of his property; all in vain. The notes of these gentlemen would be, I am afraid, to the President, some of the unpleasantest words that ever blotted paper. Nearly every fact and statement confirmed Waterboer's claims. The information then obtained and recorded has never appeared in any blue book. What, if some day it should be found in the archives of the defunct Republics?

Strange it is that this obscure spot on the banks of the Modder River, round which there gathered strife of tongues and war of words, and to which all eyes were turned in 1870, should, 30 years hereafter, be the spot on which, amidst fire and smoke, shot and shell, carnage and death, the supremacy of Britain in South Africa should tremble in the balance. Yet, so it was.

CHAPTER XXII

There was now much unrest because of the delay in issuing the report of the Commission. Every Griqua was in a state of uncertainty and suspense. The friends of the people said: "You have no cause for anxiety, your land grants will be confirmed by the Government right enough." But there were some who said the opposite, and the poor folk did not know whom to believe. The unrest was increased by the arrival in February, '76, of *C. P. Watermeyer, Esq.*, *Mr. F. Watermeyer*, *Mr. St. v. Erskine* and *Mr. C. C. Henkel* to begin a general *survey* of the country. The decision of the Government, to carry out an extended survey now taking practical shape, was opposed by Mr. Brisley and many of the leading Griquas. Their contention was thus expressed: "This is Griqualand. The Government has "undertaken to manage its affairs without introducing exten- "sive or radical changes. The Government is exceeding its "rights, and breaking its promises in commencing this general "survey, entailing heavy outlay, without the consent of the "people. Many of the farm-owners have already surveyed and "planted beacons. We are quite satisfied with these surveys, "and we object seriously to being subjected to this further "outlay." This proposed *survey* again set the country in a fever of commotion. The outcome of it all was that the Government gave an assurance that farm-owners who had already surveyed would not be called on to pay for their share of the new survey, and, I believe, the promise was faithfully kept.

As the year 1876 advanced there were reports of hostile movements, and intrigue going on, in all of which *Smith Pommer's* name was prominent. The *Committee* of 12 had exhausted itself. though it still continued to meet every month. The death of the Chief, and the burial with him of all hopes of a return to the old position, left them broken winged for oratorical flight. Several found the bottom knocked out of all their cherished hopes of advancement. Some had got other fish to fry, for they had turned *Land Agents*, and were ever running about with powers of attorney to sell erven or farms, with declarations of seller or purchaser, and often, scribe-like, with a pen stuck behind the ear. These men became quite learned in the language of the Conveyancer.

In the month of February, 1876, things began to look threatening about *Riet Vlei.* Pommer was known to be intriguing with Sidoi, a Kaffir chief *Mr. Donald Strachan*, who was now magistrate at Umzimkulu, had warned *Mr. Cumming*, and he had duly informed the Government, requesting that a company of the F.A.M.P. might be sent up.

In April *Capt. Blyth*, the distinguished Resident among the Fingos, was appointed to supersede T. A. Cumming. Mr. Brownlee doubtless considered *Capt. Blyth* the best man to send up to meet the contingency of an outbreak, an opinion in which many who knew the Griqus did not share from the beginning. *Capt Blyth* approached Kokstad, supported by a company of the F.A M P., in the belief that every Griqua was disloyal and prepared to fight. This misapprehension of the position was productive of much of the unhappy history immediately following. The report of his approach reached Kokstad on a Sunday morning. Mails were few and of telegrams there were none. Blyth expected the Griquas, if they were friendly disposed, to go out and *meet him.* Most of the Griquas attended divine service. In those days, I doubt, if they would have gone to meet the Queen herself if she had chosen to visit them on a Sunday morning. And so it came about that not a single Griqua went out to welcome the Captain. He took it as a sign of hostility, in spite of all *Mr. Cumming's* assurances to the contrary, and he was at no pains to conceal his chagrin.

The Griquas were familiar with his name; had heard of his iron but successful rule of the Fingos, and of their complete submission to his strong will. Blyth came to Kokstad with the military spirit which said: "I'll make these upsetting Griqua fellows knuckle down, you'll see" The Griquas on the other hand met him saying to themselves: "Does this fire-eater think that he is to order us about and deal with us as if we were Kaffirs?"

Capt. Blyth entered the town and encamped. His strong language, the presence of so many armed men, the waggons with ammunition, the military precautions of mounting guard, etc., were all to the Griquas like so many menaces of hostility. They were already suspicious of Blyth, and Blyth was equally suspicious of them. Espionage on both sides followed and increased the suspicion.

Next day Capt. Blyth "took over" from *Cumming.* He immediately issued orders for a general muster of the burghers, and in a few days the town was full. As usual, the Griquas came armed and mounted, a circumstance which added to Capt. Blyth's suspicions and led to further military precautfons. In the centre of the Market-square a pole was planted and the Union Jack run up. Underneath it Capt. Blyth took his stand and read his commission. He told the Griquas that he had reason to believe treason was rampant among them; that he had come to put all that down, and he would do it. He would administer justice with perfect fairness and impartiality, but he would put down all treasonable talk with a high hand. The *Committee of 12*, he considered, was a treasonable body, and he would henceforth prohibit its meetings. They were now subjects of the Queen, and they must be loyal to the flag which waved over them. He then intimated that he had brought with him printed *lists* of all the *land grants* approved by the Government, and these were distributed broadcast. One of the Griquas inquired if he might be permitted to ask a question. "Certainly," said the Captain. "Well," said he, "I "wish to know if it be the custom of the Queen of England to "demand allegiance from an unwilling people? Does "she now-a-days annex a people in THE SAME way as you "catch game? Are we annexed by might or right?" The Captain's answer to these questions was not in the most gentle terms, and in substance was something as follows: "You see that flag? there it is, the symbol of sovereignty, justice, protection, freedom to all who are under it. How or why you were annexed is a matter with which I have nothing to do. All I know is that you are British subjects, and while you enjoy the privileges you must accept the responsibilities, so there is an end to that talk." Such was, in substance, the issue of Captain Blyth's first tussle with the Griquas, and such the speech held when the old flag was, for the first time, hoisted. Sullen of face and angry at heart the Griquas went home that afternoon. One might have heard them ringing changes on the old grievances: "*Taken over like sheep*," "*Forty years money unsettled*," "*Treaty trampled on*," "*What about our Volksraad and Griqua law?*" "*Mensche, dit is zwaar*" (Sirs, this is hard). Their pride received a wound that day which has never quite healed up.

This brings me now to the saddest episode in the early annals of the town. Gladly woulp I omit reference to it, but subsequent events would be inexplicable in the absence of a faithful statement of what occurred on the evening of this day.

The *lists of confirmed land grants* were now in the hands of the people. They had been printed, as usual, the family name first, the christian name following. The method was new to the Griquas, and hence each one failed to find his name in the list of grants approved. This was taken as confirmatory of what had been bruited about that Government would break faith with them. Night had now come on; there was no one to explain, and, indeed, they were in no mood to reason. *Mr. Cumming* was preparing to leave with his family. The writer, in whom, I venture to think, most of them would have had confidence, was in King William's Town on church business. Almost without exception they were feeling hurt, humiliated, or angry. Wherever it had come from, there was undoubtedly liquor in the town that night. Some of the supply had reached *Willem Kok*, son of the wife of the late chief This man accounted himself, notwithstanding the discreditable accident of his birth, "*een geboren koning*" (every inch a king) When a drop of spirits reached his brain he did and said the wildest things. In the twilight of this eventful evening Willem stood in the "Palace yard." The F.A.M.P. were marching up the street escorting the ammunition wagon. With his measured step and slow, long stick in hand, "*Toll*" (his familiar name) walked across the street. Now whether "*Toll*" was too eager to give or the men too ready to take offence will probably never be known. But a F.A.M.P. trooper affirmed that "Toll" lifted his hand to assault him. "Toll" said they needlessly rode down upon him and he lifted his arm to turn aside the horse's head. At any rate, a hue and cry was raised that "a Griqua had assaulted the Police." The men stood to arms. The Captain and officers in command were hurriedly fetched from dinner in a high state of excitement. In a few minutes there was a huge fuss all over the street. Recriminations and angry words followed from all sides. It was now dark; most of the Griqua people were in their houses poring over the *lists*, and in some cases talking loudly and violently. *Captain Blyth* gave the order *to search every Griqua home, and to seize all firearms.* In vain *Mr. Cumming* tried to dissuade him from this course; he was inexorable. He had been offended at the lack of attention, the questions, and the attitude of the people. He believed they had hostile intentions. "Four of his five wits went a halting." Search was made by excited and angry troopers Quiet, staid, harmless old men were knocked up in the middle of the night to deliver up their fire-arms. The night visit and the demand confirmed their worst fears. Some refused to open and the door was broken in. Old *Titus Klein*, the original owner and occupier of the present printing house, a most inoffensive old slaveman, one of Kok's very best councillors, was pulled out of his house struggling in the dark and pretty roughly handled. *E. Stafford*, a European storekeeper, from Natal, who was present, cried out: "Shame, don't strike the man when he is down." Captain Blyth, who was also there, replied: "Who are you?" "I am Edward Stafford, sir." "Well, you come to my office to-morrow morning at 10 o'clock and I will talk to you." "I will, sir." Inside the house, the women screamed and extinguished the light. The police entered, relighted, and searched the place with no gentle hand. Titus was arrested and detained till next morning. When he returned he found his furniture scattered about, his boxes opened, and his ready cash amounting to £4 gone. While this was going on here, another company had obtained forcible entrance to the "Palace." It was occupied only by the chief's widow, her female attendants, and a few boys. The police ransacked the house, disturbed the old lady, who was a confirmed invalid, turning even the bedding up side down in search of concealed fire-arms.

Next morning there was no small excitement. The leading Griquas appeared protesting in firm but respectful language against the treatment they had received, affirming their innocence of any thought of hostility or resort to arms. They appealed to Mr. Cumming. He declined to take any action beyond expressing his confidence in them and regret that *Captain Blyth* had not acted on his advice.

Stafford appeared at the office to receive the due reward of his deeds, and received instead an expression of regret amounting to an apology. The chief's widow with her attendants, and also the *Jood* family, were all busy packing their wagons to trek to Natal "*for safety,*" and they went at once. The Griquas were gathering in groups recounting to one another, doubtless with some exaggeration, the events of the night before A new grievance was added to the old stock. The satirical remark was often made then and repeated after: "*This is what our minister must mean when he speaks of the privileges of British citizenship! We don't like it.*" As the day advanced *Mr. Cumming* and *Mr. Barker* and others were able to explain to the more ignorant the meaning of the reversed names on the land lists. When they found that, after all, the grants of Adam Kok were confirmed, this became an excellent plaster for their sores. Captain Blyth became more conciliatory. There is reason to believe that the Captain was beginning to see how things actually were, and to realize that he had got a set of people to manage very different from the obsequious Fingos. *Widow Kok* went to the village of *Harding*, in Natal, and remained there for several weeks until Captain Blyth got her son-in law persuaded to go and bring her back.

I have described what took place, not from personal observation, but from the reports of many witnesses—some Griquas on whose veracity I could depend, as well as from such men a Cumming, Stafford and Barker.

During my absence reports of these things appeared in the King William's Town press. It was impossible for me to return at once. Feeling that I had a duty to the people to discharge, I sat down and wrote a *Dutch letter* to the Griquas and had it printed, sent up and circulated. Unfortunately, in the great haste and from the printer's ignorance of the language, many typographical errors crept in and were over-looked, but it placed before them specifically the points which I had so frequently made the subjects of public and private teaching: That civil government is of divine appointment; that Providence had now clearly placed them under Colonial rule; that their interest and safety lay in accepting British citizenship loyally; that the Government meant to do what was right and fair; and generally invoking confidence in the good faith of the Government. The pamphlet which bore the title "*Friendly Counsel to a Perplexed People*," was considered by outsiders to have served a good purpose. There were some irreconcilables who, when they read or heard read the pamphlet, said: "Let us hang the minister on the nearest tree as soon as he returns." But the hanging did not come off. Some time thereafter I was surprised and pleased to have sent to me a cheque covering the cost of publication.

This is perhaps the best place to refer to the character of *Captain Blyth*, who had so much to do with the early history of Griqualand East. He had many excellent qualities. He was kindness itself, and delighted in noble and kindly deeds. He had an intensely tender heart, and was generous to a fault. He was honourable, upright, sincere. He said exactly what he meant, and meant exactly what he said. He had a hot temper, but was placable, and could forgive and forget, and he expected others to do the same. Unfortunately, he often acted first and considered afterwards. He meant always to do what he believed to be right and best. He was the friend of the coloured man in every fibre of his nature. He meant well with the Griquas, and the proofs of his goodwill are manifold. He was unsparing of their faults, especially their thriftless, wasteful ways, their lack of energy and industry. He was so intensely loyal himself that he could not brook or forgive the halting and hesitant loyalty of those who objected to become good subjects even by a stroke of the pen or the fluttering of a piece of cotton in the wind. He knew more of justice and equity than he did of law. He was a splendid soldier, a bad diplomatist, a first-rate dictator, a poor tactician The submission and obedience he demanded was more that of a soldier than of a citizen. If T. A Cumming was John Bull's hand in the velvet glove, Captain Blyth's was the same but with steel mail under. It is excellent to have a giant's strength, but tyrannous to use it as a giant. He defeated his own purpose among the Griquas by too much flag flying, too much beating the big drum and hanging up the cat before them. Give him a people like the Fingos, trustful, pliable, almost cringing and *Captain Blyth* could do anything he liked with them. Set him over a people like the *Griquas as they then were*, proud, self-confident, diplomatic, and his pot would boil over before he took thought of his position.

The mistake he made on that April night in 1876 was largely atoned for by subsequent conciliatory action and excellent service. By the irreconcilables, however, *Ledowick*, *Adam Muis*, *Smith Pommer*, etc., the events of that night were never forgotten or forgiven, and became the kernel of a lasting grievance, ultimately culminating in bloodshed.

The Committee of 12 was now suppressed. Captain Blyth acted in perfect good faith, but he made a huge blunder It was bad policy and bad government, because arbitrary and illegal. Liberty to meet and talk is to the Griqua a healing plaster for all sores. Gag him and his wounds fester.

Let us look at the exceedingly anomalous position Captain Blyth took up. The Chief was dead, the Volksraad not summoned, the Committee suppressed. Blyth demanded allegiance. The people said: "Allegiance! To whom? The Queen's authority "has never been declared supreme. There is no document to "show that she claims our allegiance. No letters patent have been "issued sanctioning annexation, no parliamentary sanction has been "proclaimed No proclamation exists, except the bit of paper "read on 16th October, and that bears no signature. Is this the "doing of the Queen or the Governor or the Parliament? If we "are to be obedient, to what law? Griqua Law? It is ignored. "Colonial law? We don't know it. Is Captain Blyth a law to "himself? Where are we now?"

The fact is there was a kind of interregnun of authority. Captain Blyth was really *dictator*, exercising autocratic power, and the only law was that of *Salus Populi*. But all this the politicians and demagogues and agitators among the Griquas did not and could not understand. The unique position gave them material for the manufacture of grievances and fomenting of disaffection

After some weeks *Mrs. Kok* returned. The Griquas found their land grants confirmed. They laid aside their suspicion and fears, and the bulk of them settled down to acquiesce in the new regime. Captain Blyth tried to meet their wishes in every way, put himself to infinite trouble to find out their laws and customs in the administration of justice He did much useful service, fixing boundaries of farms and locations, road making, improvement of the town, erecting *pro tem* offices and jail, investigating and settling the debts of the old Government, recognising and paying out arrears of the Forty Years money. He was continually at work, and did not spare himself. He brought his wife and children to the town. *r Blyth*, with her charms of manner, gracious disposition, and social qualities, greatly aided him. Together they formed admirable social leaders for the little growing European community.

CHAPTER XXIII.

The Frontier Armed and Mounted Police pitched their tents on the ground now occupied by the Roman Catholic buildings. As the months went on they substituted small huts of sod for their tents. They were very irregularly placed, and were wondrous structures both for variety of material and style of architecture – fearfully and wonderfully made. The doors were ornamented with scraps of commercial literature, such as: "This side up," "Glass, with care," "Keep clear of the boilers," "T O. Hall." A wag, bent on improving the occasion, made these into: "To HELL. KEEP CLEAR OF THE SPOILERS. TAKE A GLASS WITH CARE." I found last year one of the original huts still standing at the back of the

Roman Catholic premises against the "Stony Kopie." It is one of the relics of the original police camp The men were lonely enough in their little huts, and had few opportunities of relaxation. I gave them the use of the large Griqua School room for a Concert, and also the use of my piano. Alas! I brought a hornets nest about my ears. The concert was just such as a lot of rollicking young fellows would get up, concluding with Christy Minstrels, in which clever and original jokes at Griqua expense were freely introduced. O, dear me! didn't I catch it? "*The English have taken our* "*country, displaced our Volksraad, and now they come into our own* "*buildings, blacken their faces and make fun of us.*" The young fellows saw their mistake, and were sorry to have brought me into trouble. It took an infinite amount of talking and bushels of somewhat shaky logic to quiet some of the fiery Griqua spirits. After that somewhat bitter experience I had to forbid in the School-room all Christy Minstrels or any comic song in character which might tread on tender toes. This first concert had one very serious practical outcome. It dried up the sources from whence had to come the contributions for the completion of the Griqua church. "No," said the Griquas, "we will not subscribe another shilling. "Whose property will it ultimately become? The English have "taken our country, what is to hinder them to take the church "next? We have not forgotten the concert and the black faces." From that time I had to borrow money to complete the work. O, ye ladies and gentlemen of Kokstad, who at your ease in your beautiful hall delight the citizens with your musical performances, ye little know what painful memories are associated with the first introduction of these feasts of reason and this flow of song There are a few still left who can remember the boisterous mirth, the somewhat discordant jingling of the old home-tuned piano and Sergt-Major Birbeck singing "The Old Grenadiers," all joining in the chorus till the welkin rang again.

THE CONCERT.

A Griqua describes in the taal the first concert held in the School-room, Kokstad, 1876 :

Veel hou de Engelsh van CONCERT,
  Hij trek de best aan.
Laat staan, al is 't de ergste smert.
  Is 't licht of donker maan.

Hij gaat er heen met vrouw en kind,
  Waar 't zingt en 't lacht en praat,
Is hul voor 't speelen erg gezind,
  Dan blijft de speeltje laat.

Ik was rigt geerie eens te zie
  Wat dat was voor een ding
Dat mensch kan lekker geld uitgee,
  Te hoor een Rooinek zing.

Een baatje zwart met vogel stert
  Leen ik van broer Sam,
Een hempd, een shilling, van oom Gert,
  Dan was ik net oorlam.

Nu gaat ik in met trotsche gang.
  Zit op de voorste bank.
Voor deuts-olk was ik nimmer bang.
  Wat het ik hul te dank ?

De huis was vol. Ach ! dat was mooi
  Te zien zoo 'n blijde volk.
De heertjes zat elk met een nooi,
  Ik miste net een tolk.

Met speel en zang was geen verzuim,
  Geen wijse kende ik,
Maar 't vloeit al klinkend uit de duim,
  Nieuw met elk oogenblijk.

Dan volgde iets dat maakt mij naar,
  Ik zat op heete kool.
Tien zwarte kerels met LANGE HAAR,
  Elk met een soort VIOOL.

Kwam voor, en zat elk op een stoel,
  Rigt koddig aangetrek,
Een bont en aardig leelijk boel.
  Mij beefde op de plek.

Denk ik wat wil DAT nu afgee ?
  Waar kom die klomp van daan ?
Is 't Neger mensch van oer de zee ?
  Of is 't mombakjes aan ?

Mombakjes is dat waarlijk niet,
  Dat's zwartsel op de vel.
Waar 'n kerel had 't zwartsel afgevee,
  Gewaar ik Sergeant Bell.

Hul speel en dans, elk zoo 'l 's een gek.
  Tien schepsels op een rij.
'T kwam my in 't hoofd de Rooinek
  Trek schimpend pijl op mij.

De bruin man, Ach ! in eigen huis
  Te maken voor een spot !
Ik raakt onstuimig in 't gedruis,
  Net zoo 's een kookend pot.

Zweet liet ik val op dit gebouw,
  Om 'r kinders in te leer.
Nu lijkt als of een plan 's op touw
  Om ons hier uit te keer.

Bloed kruipt toch waar het niet kan gaan,
  Bij witte ook bij zwaart.
Te veel een open zeer te slaan
  Wordt onverdragelijk smart.

Men noemt dat "Christy Minstrels," nie ?
  Is toch de mensch niet schaam,
Aan zoo 'n godloos ding te gee
  Zoo lietlijk een naam ?

Several new places of business were opened about this time. *Henry Watkinson* opened a store in an out-house at the back of *Mr. Brisley's* house, in which at first *Captain Blyth* resided. This man came to Griqualand East first with a small stock of goods in a Scotch cart. He was clever, well read, respectably connected, and brimfull of humour. He was an inveterate gambler. Whether by success at the table or in business or both I know not, but he acquired wealth, speculated in land and went into farming. He was one of the characters of Kokstad during its most formative period. *Wildredge & Pringle* came in about this time from Umzimkulu, where they had traded on the spot where Strachan & Co.'s store now stand. They erected the wood and iron building opposite the Masonic Hotel. *Bydell & Uys*, two coloured men, opened a store in the Griqua brick house opposite the tower of the Griqua church. They soon prospered, bought the corner of *A. P. D. Smith's* erf and built on it, and in a very short time had Shop, Bakery, Butchery, Mail Contract, Jail Contract, Police Contract. By-and-by they opened a Canteen and Billiard Room, which, I fear, proved ultimately their ruin. Both Billiard Room and Canteen certainly brought ruin to many of the Griquas. *John Hill* bought the original little mill and improved and worked it while erecting his *turbine* on the present site. He received permission from Mr. Brownlee, S. N. Affairs in 1877, to utilize the water of the Umzimhlava and construct the long furrow through the town lands. Captain Blyth resided for some time in Brisley's house, but began to construct his own at the north end of the town. We considered the site he selected quite outside the town, almost in the country. The Government took over the building, and it served as *Government House* till the present *Residence* was built. Resident Magistrates were now appointed at *Matatiele, Umzimkulu, Mount Frere*. Captain Blyth became *Chief Magistrate*. Griqualand East at first included the three districts of Mount Curric, Umzimkulu and Matatiele. Now its boundaries were extended to embrace the districts now included in the designation Griqualand East. I mention this because it made *Kokstad* the seat of a *Chief Magistracy* and vastly increased its political importance. As a consequence of this movement, the offices of Chief Magistrate and Resident Magistrate were separated. *Mr. G. W. Hawthorne* became first Resident Magistrate of Kokstad. *E. Barker* was now clerk to the Chief Magistrate and Postmaster.

Mr Harry Ford came up along with Captain Blyth to establish a *Deeds Registry*, but as no titles had been issued no transfers could be effected, no mortgage bonds passed. His office became a sinecrue, and he gave up his time to assist where help was most needed. He remained until Captain Blyth was moved in 1878, and is now Master of the Supreme Court, Kimberley.

In the second company of the F.A.M.P. there came a young man *Frank Compton*. He had almost completed his course of study for M.D. The men of his troop gladly availed themselves of his skill, and very soon his services were in requisition in the town and district. He was relieved from garrison duty, and gave his time to the relief of the sick, military and civil. My dispensary was placed at his disposal, and he rendered most valuable public service. This service he continued until the arrival of *Dr. Guild* in the beginning of 1879. He received a public testimonial and purse of money, and when his period of service had expired he went to Australia, where he became a prosperous sheep farmer. His name deserve honourable mention in the roll of Kokstad benefactors and founders.

CHAPTER XXIV.

I have mentioned in another connection the arrival of the Surveyor *C. P. Watermeyer* and his staff. Mr. Watermeyer was selected by Mr. Brownlee because of his professional skill, and, perhaps, more because of his sterling rectitude, his kindly disposition towards coloured men, and his knowledge of Dutch. He set to work almost immediately by laying down with marvellous accuracy his *base line* on the Umzimvubu flats. The progress of the work was greatly retarded by the unrest of the following years. He was fortunate in having as his draughtsman a gentleman who was also a photographer, Mr. C. C. Henkel. He produced a set of photographs of the completed map showing every line, beacon and road, as well as the detailed features of the country. I believe I am expressing the opinion of experts in saying that the quality and accuracy of the work done in connection with the survey has not been excelled in any district of South Africa. Griqualand East is under lasting obligations to the late Mr. Watermeyer and his staff for the patience, devotion and skill they brought to their several tasks.

Very soon after the Surveyors began their work a *Land Board* was created. It consisted of Blyth, Watermeyer, Barker and Hawthorne. The Griquas were requested to choose a representative. They chose *Klaas v d. Westhuizen*—an unfortunate and absurd selection. The duties of this Board were to consider fresh applications for farms and erven, to settle boundries of farms and locations, and generally to supplement the work of the Commission of the previous year. I have stated elsewhere the principles of land distribution. The proposal to reserve fhe *Locations* for the Basutos and Kaffirs, as nearly as possible as Captain Kok had left them was to the Griquas the unpardonable sin of the Government. Their idea was: " If a Griqua sells his farm and becomes landless why should he not have another farm cut out from the location grounds, get title to it and let the Kaffirs or Basutos become tenants or 'bywooners.' " The root idea of feudalism dies hard !

This, of course, was out of the question, but it was by such absurd claims that the Griquas injured their best interests and alienated the sympathy of their best friends. The Land Board had

Mr. T. A. Cumming.

Rev. W. Murray.

CAPTAIN M. SMYTH

most difficult work to do. Doubtless they made minor mistakes, but they meant to do their perplexing work with fairness and impartiality, and generally they were successful In saying this much I am well aware that I lay myself open to the ill-will of some, especially Griquas, who take quite an opposite view ; but having had opportunity of observation and research I have no hesitation in bearing this testimony. Had the Griquas selected as their representative a man of greater intelligence and weight of character their interests could not have received greater consideration, but they would have become acquainted with the reasons for the Board's decision in each case.

When it was decided that a particular applicant for land was entitled to it, the Land Board issued *a certificate* to that effect. Hundreds of these *rights* were sold at once, sometimes before the ink was well dry. The seller got his money, and had no further claim. All his right passed over to the purchaser, who now personally or by deputy visited all unallotted lands and made his selection. The seller soon got rid of his money, but somehow could not get over the conviction that *he* only got "*a piece of paper*" while the *purchaser* by and by came into possession of the broad acres. The agitator and the demagogue were always ready to say : "*Yes, that is because you are coloured and he is white.*" This wild mad selling of *rights* was productive of much dissatisfaction. Yet none were to blame but the sellers themselves. They would take no warning. They became wise only when it was too late.

CHAPTER XXV.

Early in 1877 a small party of Dutch *Boers* settled around the Umzimvubo Drift. At the request of their Predikant I visited them, and ministered to them as time and strength permitted. These early settlers—*De Bruin*, *Van Dyk*, *Sutherland*, *Klopper*, &c.—were joined by others, until the district around the Drift became almost entirely occupied by Dutch. I continued this work until 1891, when they were able to get a minister of their own. During the 14 years of my acting pastorate I visited them monthly, conducting service, baptizing, holding Sacrament, and marrying. During this time the Township of *Cedarville* was laid out, the first Dutch Church built and paid for, and steps taken to secure a Manse. The Township was laid out by *Watkinson and Caldecott*. A site for a Church and £100 was given as an inducement to the Boers to purchase Erven. Many objected to the site, but none other offered.

During the months of 1875-6 the work of building the

Griqua Church proceeded steadily. I personally superintended the whole work, which was all done by Griqua workmen until we came to the tower. For work done on it they demanded unreasonable wages, and ever increasing as the *danger increased with the height.* I have elsewhere referred to the difficulty of feeding the workmen and how that was got over. For the paying of them we had the Free State money available. When that was exhausted I collected a good deal among the Griquas. I cannot remember how much, but it must have been several hundreds of pounds. More funds would have been forthcoming, for money was now plentiful, but for the tacit conviction that, by hook or crook, the English would ultimately get possession of the building. At last we had to borrow up to £500, which was the sum due when the building was opened, May, 1877. Of this, £300 was paid off at the opening services, and £200 remained. Promises for that amount were given, to be paid off within six months, but the events of the following year made the recovery of the promised sums difficult, in some cases impossible.

The completion and opening of the Griqua Church was a great event in the history of the town and a red letter day in the Griqua calendar. While the event was cause of rejoicing it was not without its sorrows. It had been arranged a month before that my eldest daughter should perform the ceremony of opening the door. When the time came her bright joyous spirit had gone where no temple is needed. An attack of inflamation of the lungs baffled medical skill, proved fatal, and caused a great blank not only in my family circle, but, I may truly add, in the social circle of the little town.

Then, only a week or so thereafter, Mr. Walsh, the carpenter, who had come up from Richmond to build the staircase, sickened of the same ailment and died. These events cast a gloom over the community and moderated the joy felt, especially by the Griqua people, on the completion of this great undertaking. Six years had passed since the foundations had been laid.

The widow of the chief was now asked to turn the key, which she did on the day of opening.

There were present and took part Revs. Birt from Peelton; J. Harper, King Williamstown; F. Kayser, Knaaps Hope; W. Murray, from Ugie; and John Feruie, from Natal.

The collection at the first service held in the new building amounted to £180, and the gatherings at the series of functions totalled £300. The balance of £200 was raised by mortgage bond, and paid off with small difficulty during the following years of war and disquiet.

During 1875 I began in the school-room an English service, which was fairly well attended. This service was kept up during my absence in England in 1877-78, by the help of friends, and specially Mr. C. C. Henkel, Draughtsman to the Survey. It was resumed on my return, and issued in the organization of the present English Congregational Church in Kokstad. Both congregations used the same building at different hours, until the present Congregational Church was erected and opened in the beginning of 1891.

In May, 1877, after 12 years' absence, I went to the Home country for rest and change. During my absence occurred the outbreak which I now proceed to describe and record.

One word first regarding the position of the chief actors. *Smith Pommer* had again been secretly fomenting disaffection amongst his party at Rietvley, and it is believed he was intriguing with Sidoi. Smith had seen his power go down and Donald Strachan's star arise. His pride was wounded, his influence curtailed, his balloon pricked. He was bent on revenge.

Lodowijk Kok had been some years absent in Griqualand West, and now returned to find the chief of his house dead, and a *Kok* on the same level as ordinary mortals. He had taken to drinking and wasted his property. He was full of self reproach, and had no end of grievances against every-one in Church and State.

His brother, *Adam Muis*, who had waited long for dead men's shoes without getting them, was an impoverished and disappointed candidate for Royal honours. When a man has high notions, disappointed hopes, exhausted exchequer, blasted credit, no trade at his finger ends, no moral balance or divine grace, a traditional aversion to honest toil, and like the steward in the parable, feels "I cannot dig, and to beg I am ashamed," desperation easily makes him the devil's dupe. He must needs go whom the devil drives.

A. P. D. Smith had been the moving spirit in the *Committee of* 12. He took no part in the outbreak, but he helped materially *to create the atmosphere of discontent, which made it possible and easy*. He was a "*Kapenaar*," came to the country in 1868 in the humble capacity of cook and valet to the chief. He could speak and write English inperfectly. He was the relative of Adam Muis's wife, son-in-law of Rev.

Hans Bezuidenhout, was closely allied to officers in *esse* or in *posse* in Church and State. During Adam Kok's lifetime he was a *nobody*. After his death he made a bid for popularity and *leadership*. He revelled in Committees, Reports, Memorials and Protests. He was a kind of chronic protestant. He largely helped to keep the political pot boiling, and so contributed to its boiling over. In all fairness to this man, who was the most extraordinary moral mixture I have ever known, I have to record that while he was the best grumbler in the congregation, he was also the most diligent and useful Sunday School Teacher.

On the 20th February, 1878, *Lodowijk Kok* entered the store of *Wildridge & Pringle*, and somewhat imperiously demanded to be served. Pringle declined to serve him if he persisted in speaking in such a disrespectful manner. Angry words followed. Pringle ordered him off the premises. Lodowijk refused to go and Pringle persisted in turning him out. A scuffle ensued. Adam Muis appeared on the scene and took sides with his brother. The police landed both brothers in jail. Next morning *Adam Muis* was released on bail, *Lodowijk* retained to await his trial. Muis, deeply mortified and vowing vengeance, went off to Pondoland. There he induced about 94 Pondos, under *Josiah Jenkens*, to espouse his cause. These marched armed to the border at *Brook's Neck*, where they were joined by a number of disaffected Griquas. They crossed the neck, and began to commit depredations. They arrested a Mr. Acutt, and kept him prisoner in his own house while they helped themselves to what they wanted. Next day they marched in a circuitous route past Salzer's & Gunther's, and encamped in the ruined houses of the old Laager. Meantime Pommer's party were assembling from *Under Zuurberg*, plundering wagons and helping themselves to horses on the way. The Pondo contingent, as soon as they came in sight of Kokstad, thought better of it, deserted Muis, rode into Kokstad, and gave themselves up to Blyth. Muis and Pommer now demanded a "*Vergadering*" or public meeting with Captain Blyth, making it a condition that they should "meet him armed." To this the Captain replied that he would discuss no grievance with men in arms, that they had been guilty of disturbing the peace, and he demanded immediate surrender or he would attack them in so many hours. On Sunday morning early, 14th April, Blyth sent *Abraham Jantjes*, an old Griqua, much respected and trusted, to make a final effort to induce them to give in. He met with some rough treatment and had some difficulty in returning. About midday Blyth attacked, and in a short, sharp engagement routed the insurgents. *Adam Mais* stood at bay on the western flank of Mount Currie, and was shot. While the engagement was going on Sidoi and his Kafirs appeared over the neck on the eastern spur of the mountain. *Donald Strachan* rode out, took them in hand, and succeeded in landing them in a safe place, disarming them, and placing them under guard. There is little doubt *Sidoi* was in league with Smith Pommer, although ostensibly coming to support his Magistrate Strachan. As soon as Pommer saw Sidoi under Strachan's command, he fled with most of his followers, and did not stop till he reached Rietvley.

The little town was now in a state of siege. The loyal population, white and black, had moved into an entrenched Laager or Fort, which stood near the present site of the Government School. In the centre was the *Powder* Magazine, the tents ranged around. Guards were set and the drifts watched night after night for some eight days while all this was going on. The battle took place on a Sunday afternoon, and was all over by four o'clock. The victors returned elated with triumph, and were gathered inside the Fort. Suddenly, without the least warning, the Magazine exploded. The building with its contents, stone, brick, wood, iron, cartridges and the guns taken from the Pondos were all blown in the air. The two guards inside were blown literally to atoms. Eight persons were killed outright, several were wounded, all were stunned, blinded and dazed. The sound of the explosion was heard 30 miles distant.

Captain Blyth, who happily escaped uninjured, took immediate steps for the safety of the Garrison throwing up temporary entrenchments where the walls of the Fort had been blown down, and seeing to the careful collection and use of what ammunition was found to be left. An anxious night was passed. The return of the enemy was a grave possibility, and the attitude and temper of Sidoi's Kafirs was not encouraging. The destruction of the Magazine had deprived them of the means of selfdefence.

The following is a list of the dead :—

Mr. J. H. Pringle, son of the Provost of Leith, Scotland.

Mr. George Stafford, clerk to D. Strachan, Magistrate.

Mr. James Ellis, Bricklayer.

Miss. M. Watermeyer, daughter of the Surveyor.

Mrs. Uijs, wife of a coloured shopkeeper.

A German orphan girl, nurse to Mr. Henkel's children.

Two Privates of the F.A.M.P., names unknown.

The mangled bodies of the dead were hurriedly buried. For several days the shattered remains of the men who had been inside were picked up within a radius of several hundreds of yards from the scene of the disaster, and, without any attempt at recognition, interred. *Mr. Pringle* was killed outright, so also was *Miss Watermeyer.* The grave of the former is in the cemetery, the grave of the latter is under the willows at the S.E. corner of the Market Square.

Many and various are the causes alleged for this catastrophe. Some alleged *treachery*, but this is more the nature of a surmise. One eyewitness asserted that the guard was intoxicated. Certain it is that large quantities of liquor had been brought to the Fort, and it was too easily accessible. Another eyewitness affirmed that the guard was seen smoking his pipe inside on a powder barrel. Most people ascribe the accident to the careless handling of the Pondo guns while being deposited, some say "thrown" into the Magazine. These are theories. The only men who knew were blown to pieces.

Meantime a price of £100 was set on Pommer's head, dead or alive. On the morning of the 17th April *Donald Strachan* and a detachment of F.A.M.P. and Kafirs set out to intercept *Pommer* and his party, who were known to be making for Pondoland along the crest of the Ingeli Mountain. They were sighted at the mouth of a wooded gorge, over against the farm "The Wolds." Hostilities opened at once. Pommer was shot high up in the kloof. The others tried to escape down the precipitous and almost pathless glen, through the thick underwood. One by one they were cut down by the Kafirs following close on their heels. Only a very few escaped to Pondoland. The body of *Pommer* was brought into Kokstad lashed on a led horse, and buried in the corner of the Government Erf close up against the grave of Adam Kok. The Kafir who fired the fatal shot and his companions, generously waived their claim to the money reward, on condition that it should be given to the widow of Mr. G. Stafford, Strachan's clerk and assistant, who had been killed in the explosion.

The bodies of the dead Griquas lay in the wooded kloof, unburied, from April till December, when the writer, *H. Watkinson* and *Ed. Barker* organised a burial party and interred them. Among the fallen was Johannes Albrecht, brother-in-law to Pommer. He was a man of splendid physique and of high moral worth—honest, industrious, gentle, generous, a thoroughly good, worthy man. How Pommer could have persuaded that man to join in his mad schemes will remain a mystery till the great day of revelation. His good wife, who had been a servant in my family, never believed he was dead until I fetched from off his skeleton lying in a pool of cold water in the kloof, pieces of the clothing she had made with her own hands. Poor girl, she herself had running in her veins blood from an ancient historic and noble English family. How pathetic is life to some of God's creatures!

Within a few days after the engagement at Ingeli, the insurrectionists were either caught or gave themselves up. They were marched to Durban, shipped there to Capetown, and confined in the Amsterdam Battery.

The men who took sides with Muis and Pommer were not the more respectable and worthy of the Griqua people. For instance, there was not a single officer of the Griqua Church among them, and only a very few accredited members of it. They were the less intelligent and more excitable members of the community, and those who, having failed to take out their farm grants in Kok's time, now had to wait till the survey of the country showed the authorities what land was still available for distribution amongst those who had got none. They had lost faith in the Government, and held an open ear to the Irreconcilables.

Soon after the departure of the Griqua prisoners a public meeting decided to collect money for the erection of an hospital, to be *a memorial of those who had met their death in the terrible explosion*, and some progress was made. The Zulu War and then the Basuto outbreak came in the way, and the scheme lay in abeyance. The original idea was enlarged, so that the Hospital became commemorative of those, also belonging to the District, who fell in the Basuto rising.

CHAPTER XXVI.

The Griqua prisoners, nearly 200 in number, were now airing their heels in idleness in the Amsterdam Battery in Capetown. Questions were being raised as to their exact legal position, questions more easily asked than answered. Were they, after all, British subjects? A few of them were such by birth. Had the others accepted allegiance? If so, when? Not one of them had taken the oath. Had the Queen's supremacy over them been proclaimed? If so, when? By whose authority? If they became British subjects by occupying Nomansland, ceded by Treaty from Faku to the Queen, why had they been forced into the necessity of assuming and exercising sovereign rights in the absence of any other organised form of Government? Why first compel them to establish their own form of Government, then suppress it and supplant it by no other, except the arbitrary will of one single individual, even though he should have been an angel from heaven instead of a military man accustomed only to military ways? If they were "*Rebels*" let them be brought to trial, and if found guilty, punished. Could they be brought to trial? What Court had jurisdiction? Were these people to be confined there for ever, or were they to wait till the Annexation Bill could be passed by the approaching session of Parliament, and tried by some exceptional forensic pretext, making the law reflexive? Could that be done? Would it be strictly just to try men for breaking laws which had no existence at the time?

The whole position bristled with problems for the jurist.

The late Saul Solomon had been Agent for A. Kok and his Government, and continued to take a lively interest in the people. He was by study, and long experience, a Colonial statesman, accustomed to deal with the involved questions continually springing up in our Colonial dealings with semi-independent tribes on our border. Mr. Solomon saw at once that something was wrong, and resolved to have a test case brought before the Supreme Court. *Advocate Stockenstroom* took the case in hand. The Court declared that the Government had no legal right to detain these men for a single day, and ordered their immediate release. What applied to the two cases tested, applied to all the others. The Government sent all the prisoners back by sea to East London, thence marching them to Kokstad. The Government had to cry *peccavi*, and occupied rather a humiliating position.

I am not here to be understood as laying the blame on *Captain Blyth*. The Captain was the victim of circumstances. He was placed in a false, indeed, an impossible position from the first. Our whole dealings with these people from first to last had been one series of blunders. First, we make them a sovereign people, and make them confederates and allies, and enter into treaty obligations with them. Then, by the establishment of the Queen's sovereignty north of the Orange River in 1848, we as good as make them British subjects. Six years thereafter, by the abandonment of the Sovereignty and the declaration, "*we have no interests north of the Orange River,*" we unmake their British citizenship, and make no other definition of their position. We first make Treaties with them, then without even the fermality of proclamation, declare the Treaties annulled We first fight the Boers in their defence, then declare the Treaties annulled, and secretly hand them over to the tender mercies of the same Boers. Then we find for them a new Location on British Territory. They are again to be British subjects undər a Birtish Magistrate. We fail to fulfil our promises. No Magistrate appears, and they have to rule themselves. We leave them in miserable uncertainty as to whether they are British or not Again they are to all intents a sovereign people, and yet that not. Then we "annex" and don't annex. We undertake to rule them for a time under their own law and trample their own law under foot, and introduce no other. They are a people fond of diplomacy and talk. We suppress the right of public meeting, and gag them, or try to We imprison them for insurrection, and find we have no legal right. The fact is the whole attitude and conduct of the Government justified "the dominant feeling that they were free men to-day and British subjects to-morrow." The policy of sliding in can be recommended neither for its dignity nor success. It surrounded authority with an appearance of vacillation and weakness, where an attitude, in substance firm, but in manner conciliatory, might have been attended with happier results. The doctrine of a great Englishman is at all times recommended to the feelings of a childish, uneducated people, "I love the powers that be when they *be* powers" Surely here was a rumble and tumble and jumble of things.

Responsible Government had just been established at the Cape. It tried its prentice hand at annexation—the traditional pastime of Grandfather John Bull—tried it on the Griquas, of all the people in the world, and, of course, made rather an awkward job of the business. By falling we learn to walk, even along the paths of Imperialism. Best Governments sometimes, like best men, are moulded out of faults.

It is unreasonable to insist on allegiance which has neither been admitted on the one side, nor definitely claimed on the other. If the Governor had even done as the sailors did, who, to check *Paul Kruger's* efforts to secure an outlet to the Indian Ocean, put up a board lettered large enough that he who read might learn, "THIS IS BRITISH TERRITORY," Captain Blyth might have had something to appeal to in proof of his authority. But he had nothing. Captain Blyth was sent to maintain order, and he did it as a military man would be expected to do. He left other people to consider the legality of things. He could have gained the confidence and support of every man, by exercising at the start the conciliatory spirit he showed later on. The insurgent Griquas acted like madmen and fools. They refused the advice of their best friends, and followed the leading of men who had, both before and after Kok's death, shown themselves the enemies of all social order, and they suffered in consequence. Blyth was wrong in expecting the people to knuckle down in the way he demanded. The insurgent Griquas were wrong in expecting and demanding impossibilities, and when they could not get them to take up arms.

In September, 1878, Captain Blyth was re-called, and returned to his former position in Fingoland. After a brief interval the *Hon. Charles Brownlee* took his place. When the prisoners returned they were tried by Mr. Brownlee for various offences, *under their own law*. Those who had merely shared in the outbreak were dismissed with a caution. Those who had been guilty of assault, robbery and theft were punished. The live stock, wagons and moveable property of the prisoners had all already been seized and sold by summary process. The legality of much that was done was open to debate, but no questions were raised. They suffered severely for their insubordination. Some few men who had been fairly well off came back to find all their property gone.

Late in 1878 the Government appointed D. Strachan, Esq., C. P. Watermeyer, Esq., and Robert Richards, Esq., Attorney, a Commission to *inquire into the causes of the Griqua outbreak*. The principal European residents and the more influential and intelligent Griquas felt it their duty to protest against what appeared to them the manifest incongruity of including *Strachan* and *Watermeyer* in such a Commission. Our contention was that Mr. Strachan was disqualified. (1) By his intimate connection with the late chief and the part he was supposed to have taken in administering the affairs of the Griqua Government; (2) By his having acted in a military capacity in suppressing the outbreak; (3) By the circumstance that he was an extensive purchaser of land before and after annexation, and that the loss of the land through ignorance of its value was one of the alleged causes of dissatisfaction.

No such objections could be urged against the appointment of *Mr. Watermeyer*, but his young and amiable daughter had lost her life in the explosion, which certainly was one of the results of the outbreak. It was felt that it was somewhat unreasonable to expect strict impartiality from either of them.

These objections were disregarded. The Commission sat and took voluminous evidence, and its report appeared in a Blue Book next year, 1879. It is, and always will be much regretted by all who desired the most complete impartiality, that in taking evidence regarding the events of the night on which the Griqua houses were searched for arms, the testimony of T. A. Cumming and Major Giles, Magistrate then of Harding in Natal, was not called for. They were men free from all local jealousies and fears, and eyewitnesses of all that took place.

The preparation of the report of the Commission is generally attributed to Mr. Richards, himself a trained and competent lawyer. When he comes to deal with the legal position of the Griquas he is manifestly "in the toils." He performs some clever forensic somersaults. From first to last his strictures remind one of a man trying to find his way among barbed wire entanglements. The conclusion forced on one is that if the British citizenship of the Griquas depended on all this legal rigmarole, they could have only understood and realised it by all becoming learned lawyers like himself.

CHAPTER XXVII.

Mr. Brownlee had been Secretary of Native Affairs in the first Cape Cabinet after the introduction of Responsible Government. When the Molteno Cabinet was dismissed or resigned, Mr. Brownlee, according to agreement, returned to his former position as a Civil Service officer, and after a short period of service elsewhere, became Chief Magistrate of Griqualand East. He held the office with much acceptance to the inhabitants, of all classes and colours, from 25th December, 1878, till September, 1884, when failing health compelled him to retire. He and *Mrs. Brownlee* and all the members of his family were held in the highest esteem, and deservedly so. His life-long experience in dealing with native tribes, his extensive and accurate knowledge of their history and language, his personal acquaintance and friendly relations with their great chiefs Sandilli and Kreli, and, added to all this, his sauve disposition and exhaustless patience, peculiarly fitted him for the post at this particular juncture in the history of the Territory. "He was one of those gentle ones who would use the devil himself with courtesy."

Very shortly after his appointment the Annexation Bill became law, and a code of laws was published, Courts of first instance and Courts of Appeal created, so that Mr. Brownlee occupied a totally different position from that of Captain Blyth. He had the authority of Law, of Parliament, and Letters Patent at his back. He knew exactly where he was, which Captain Blyth did not. The Griquas were permitted to meet and talk to their hearts content, which made them happy, and did no one any harm. They had also become somewhat more reasonable and practical and ceased like children to cry for the moon.

For nearly two years matters in the little town moved quietly on, disturbed, of course, by the echoes of the *Zulu War* and the political commotion in the S. A. Republic. The Land Board continued its work The Surveyors were busy plotting, mapping, beaconing Houses were built; Erven along the Main Street fetched fictitious prices; new shops sprang up on both sides of the street *Francke, Grauman, Williams, Petrie, Turton, Dold, Simeon, Darby & Tyrrell* all opened stores in addition to those established at an earlier date. "*Yanke*" *Wood* had built and opened the *Royal Hotel*, and the *Masonic* was erected on the site of an old Griqua sod-house, which had been used by the F.A.M.P officers and others, dignified by thename of "Club," and facetiously call d "*The Cremorne.*"

A branch of the *Standard Bank* was opened by Mr. Taylor, first in a tent, then in the house at the S.W. corner of the square, and subsequently in the cottage between the Griqua Church and the river.

Mr. H Fowle conducted an *Agency and Auctioneer's* business in a large room opposite the Royal, which room now forms part of *Williams'* establishment.

Mr H. Griffin, from Pietermaritzburg, was the first Attorney who began to practise, and a miserable mess he made of it both for himself and some of his clients. He occupied the house which was first the Magistrate's Court, beside the Congregational Church. Other *Agents* were *Caldecott and Watkinson, Erridge.* As I have said, nearly every Griqua who could read and write a bit dabbled in Agency, often to his own loss, and more frequently to the hurt of his clients.

Gass played the rolé of *Village Blacksmith*, hammering in the old Griqua Armoury, near Harvey & Greenacre's shop.

Pearce baked bread in Jan Bergover's house, opposite the present Post Office. He tickled the palate and emptied the pockets of the Griqua children, large and small, by his tempting confectionery.

John Hill had completed his *Turbine Mill*, built the *Mill House*, and was grinding excellent meal, and the original mill was grinding in the Kloof at Matatiela.

James Barclay and *James Davie* came up from Natal in this period to erect Francke's store, and remained to become the chief builders in the town .

A singular character came to the place, "*The old Shoemaker.*" He bought an Erf and Griqua shanty above the house of Mr. Barclay. He eschewed soap and water, made no friends, worked at his last from morn till night, lived alone, made his own meals, slept all Sunday, and gained the reputation of being a hermit and a miser. He was found one morning with his throat cut at his own fireside, and to this day no trace of the murderer has been found.

Mr. Hawthorn was transferred to the Resident Magistracy of Umzimkulu, rendered vacant by the resignation of Mr. Strachan, and John T. Wylde, Esq., took his place, and speedily gained for himself the reputation of being a just judge and an excellent lawyer.

A P D. Smith, about this time, made repeated attempts to establish a *Public Market.* His broken English and lame attempts at auctioneers' humour, however, brought on him too practical jokes, and he had to desist.

A Glee Club was established, and practisings were held in the houses of those who had pianos. Occasionally concerts were given in the Griqua School-room, which still continued the only available public hall.

A *Mr. Grierson*, an Irish gentleman of large culture and limited means, came out to join his brother who was farming at *Rathfarnham*. His wife was a lady who had moved in the highest social circles, and was by no means a stranger at the Queen's Court. Not taking kindly to farming, they came into town and opened a *Private School* for white children This was the first attempt of the kind made in Kokstad. They continued their little school until the outbreak of the Basuto War, then took fright and hurried down to Durban. Mr. Grierson is now in the service of the Irish Episcopal Church. Their presence was a distinct gain to the religious and social life of the place.

Towards the close of this period a *Literary and Debating Society* sprang into existence. It met fortnightly in the Griqua Schoolroom. The Society had for its moving spirit Mr Victor Sampson, who was then in Mr. Brownlee's office. His literary resources and scientific acquirements were willingly and liberally given for the public instruction and entertainment. He is now practising as an Advocate in Kimberley, and M.L.A. for Albany.

Religious Services were conducted in the *Griqua Church* Sunday, Dutch, 10 and 4 ; English, 12 and 7 ; at the Episcopal Church, morning and evening, by Mr. Dixon, in the building now standing beside the new handsome Church *In Kafir* first in a large room which afterwards became the chief living room of the Standard Bank dwelling house, and later on, these services were continued in the present Kafir Wesleyan Church.

Mrs. Barker continued to teach in the Griqua School until June, 1879, when *Rev. W. Murray* came from Ugie and took her place.

Such was the Kokstad we knew up to the time of the Basuto war.

CAAPTER XXVIII·

Late in September, 1880, Mr. Brownlee, Mr. D. Strachan, and Mr. Hawthorne proceeded from Kokstad to *Moteri's Kop*, the residence of Mr. M. W. Liefield, then Resident Magistrate among *Makwais'* Basutos at *Matatiela.*

The Disarmament policy and the measures being taken to enforce it, had created disaffection. These gentlemen were to make an effort to allay the unrest and to restore a confidence. No more competent officers could have attempted the task. Mr Brownlee was in low spirits. He had done his best to advise against the policy. He feared a rising. He gave himself to the present distasteful duty with magnanimous devotion and self effacement.

A great gathering of Basutos was held. The practised eyes of these men detected from the actions of the people that mischief was brewing. When the meeting was over and the Basutos had gone, apparently home, Brownlee's spies found that the Basutos were to ambuscade them on their return journey. The meeting had been held on Saturday On Sunday they waited to feel their way, taking every possible precaution against surprise. They were not quite sure of their own men. So they hoodwinked the spies who were spying the spies set them all off the track, and at midnight hastily and quietly slipped out along an unused bridle path, and escaped. Towards morning the Basutos got wind of their escape, and went after them full tilt. It was a ride for life. By daylight they were through the Umzimvubu, and on their way to Kokstad. Mr. Liefeldt escaped in the opposite direction.

Next day, when the Basutos discovered that their prey was gone, they mustered in strength, fell on the various stores in Matatiela, and wantonly plundered them. The owners and storemen had escaped just in time.

There were far larger stores of liquor stocked there than was consistent with the purposes of honest trade. These were broached and the fiery contents consumed. Thus only can we account for the mad, meaningless, wanton destruction of valuable merchandise which followed

News of the rising soon spread, and the Dutch farmers located between *Cedarville* and Matatiela hurriedly fled, helter skelter, as best they could. *Gabriel de Bruijn* and his wife, each carrying a child, and the bigger ones trotting beside them, made their escape through the long grass in the dead of night, fording the river to reach friends. All their possessions were left behind and lost, for the howl of the approaching enemy warned them against any thought of getting oxen and wagon ready, or collecting stock.

Meantime we in Kokstad had no hint of the outbreak until the forenoon of Sunday.

I had conducted my usual Dutch service from 10 till 11 30 a.m. At 12 o'clock Mr. Barker told me that Brownlee, Strachan and Hawthorne were shut up in Moteri's Kop, and in serious danger. He was going to help in sending off assistance to them Mrs. Brownlee (who worshipped with us), must not be told unless things became more serious. To those of us in the know, that Sunday afternoon was a period of painful suspense, never to be forgotten.

Next day the facts became known, and the town was in a state of intense excitement and commotion. The garrison had been withdrawn to Basutoland, the town was defenceless, and an enemy of many thousands of well-armed and mounted men was less than fifty miles distant and marching on us. Mr. Wylde called the inhabitants together, stated all he knew, and by 12 o clock 23 mounted men, as well armed as time permitted, rode out under the leadership of Mr. S. Liefeldt, with the object of relieving Mr. Brownlee and his party.

A *Committee of Safety* was appointed, who decided to entrench the Griqua Church buildings—Church, House and School, making of the Church a citadel. The members were Watkinson, John Usher, the writer and a Military gentleman Knowles, who had seen service in the American War. We received authority to spend what we thought necessary. While the others planned the work, I went round and bought up every spade, pick, sack, plank, and sheet of iron obtainable, and commandeered every male not already under arms, to labour at the defence works. Next morning we had 100 men at work. The ladies of the town cut through the sacks and sewed them up when they had been filled with earth. Ditches were cut all round, and inside these were raised thick walls of sod. Loopholes were cut out of the sod walls, planks laid on, and the sandbags piled on top. The church windows were barricaded, the tower prepared for sharpshooters, the school was converted into a temporary magazine, while an underground powder chamber was being constructed. A deep well was sunk, a shed built for the reception of stores, and a pile of firewood collected. Strongly constructed gates with entanglements were placed at the east and west ends of the road which now passes between the Griqua Church and School room. We all worked hard from early morn till late at night, Sunday and week-day, till the place was in a proper condition to withstand a siege.

Regulations, approved by the Chief Magistrate, were printed by myself and delivered into every house:—They defined the alarm signals by day and night, prescribed the articles to be kept in readiness and to be brought to the Griqua

Church in the event of attack by the enemy, and the positions inside the Church to be taken up by Europeans and Griquas, &c., &c.,

Mr Wylde organised the townsmen and those from the country who had taken refuge in town, into a *Town Guard*, who every night, for several months, provided a cordon of sentinels round the outskirts *Mr. Fowle* became, *pro tem.*, Commissariat Officer. I became Paymaster for the defence construction works until they were completed. *Mr. Watermeyer* organised a *Griqua Corps*, the *Rev. Mr. Murray* was medical officer, *Rev. Mr. Dickson* took duty in the Town Guard, and every able-bodied man in the town had some defensive duty assigned to him.

While these movements were being initiated, the relieving force proceeding to the drift had met Brownlee and his party on their way back after the exciting adventures of the night. Mr. Brownlee returned to Kokstad to take supreme command. Strachan took command in the field and remained until the war ended.

The relieving force came into touch with the Basutos at the river, and a running fight ensued, with the river between. No casualties. After a time the Basutos made off for Matatiela, and completed there the devastation they had begun, clearing the country of stock as they went.

Communication by wire with Capetown was now interrupted, yet in a few days came the information that the *Poudomisi* had risen and massacred their Magistrate Mr. Hope, and his assistants Henman and Warren. Then a little later on the news came that Mr. Welsh, the Magistrate of MacLear, his wife and family, his clerk, Cumming, Rev. B. Key, afterwards the second Bishop of St. John's and family, Mr. Leary and family, were all besieged in a small stone jail at Tsolo

Ammunition and firearms were now hurried up from Pietermaritzburg, Natal Strachan called out his loyal Kafirs. "Willoughby's" and "Baker's" Horse were enlisted in Natal.

Strachan's *Kafirs* mustered in a few days, and entered Kokstad several hundreds at a time. They came along singing in unison their war song, beating their shields all in rythmic time, making a weird, and to unaccustomnd ears, a terrible sound. More than once I felt not a little nervous when these fierce armed and mounted men, with the frenzy of war on them—some in full war-paint stood two deep round the Market Square, to receive a word of encouragement from "*Charles*" *Brownlee*, before proceeding to the front. They often outnumbered the Europeans by ten to one—yet I never heard of one of them offering insult or injuring property in the town. One night some fifty of them arrived cold and wet, for whom no tents could be provided. *Mr. Brownlee* commandeered the Griqua Schoolroom for shelter. In the ante-room was stored

Holy Trinity (Episcopal) Church,
With proposed Chancel addition in memory of Bishop Key.

Griqua Church & Manse,
With surrounding fortifications during the Basuto War.

Klaas van der Westhuizen.

Mr. Donald Strachan.

ammunition. Without the least ceremony they started a fire in the centre of the wooden floor Hearing what was going on I rescued the floor from destruction by providing a sheet of iron. Fire they would have, powder or no powder.

Strachan and *Usher* took the command of all the native levies. They crossed the Umzimvubu, drove the Basutos into Basutoland, and kept them at bay while the war lasted. In these operations the first to fall was *Edward C. Barker, jun.* He was attacked and killed while scouting on the Drakensberg. Next fell *Henry Usher*, second in command of the Kafirs, whilst he was storming a cave in the mountain. At the same time the bugler boy, McPhail, was killed. The bodies of Barker and Usher were afterwards exhumed and brought to Kokstad. The writer buried young *Barker* in the cemetery, and Usher in his father's garden at *Usherwood*, both being interred with military honours.

CHAPTER XXIX.

Kokstad now became headquarters of military operations. The families of the farmers, Dutch and English, from the districts as far as Matatiela, were all collected in the town. Every room was occupied. The Dutch were, most of them, huddled into the new Wesleyan Native Church The Griquas, who had no town houses, had to content themselves with life in the wagon or under scraps of sail. These camped out on the site of the present C.M.R. barracks.

The Military authorities took possession of the Griqua Church property, including the *big bell*. The thatch of the parsonage roof was, *by order*, pulled off, and iron substituted. Sharp axes and saws were placed in readiness to fell down every one of the full grown fruit trees of the Parsonage Garden, on a given signal. These trees were the first planted in the town, and for long its pride and glory. The call for this extreme measure, happily, never came. The necessity for all these precautions will be obvious, when I state that parties of the enemy came within seven miles of the town. Sentinels were posted at each gate at the church day and night. At the gate of the Parsonage a sentinel mounted guard, and if I or any of my family happened to go outside the gate after nightfall, he, or she, could not return without giving the pass-word. Thus, for three months, we lived in a citadel. When the possibility of attack was most imminent, and our consequent anxiety at its greatest, my youngest child was born. We kept a stretcher in readiness to convey the invalid from the parsonage to the adjoining church should necessity arise.

The reader, if he refers to the *Graphic* of 1880, will find an illustration of the parsonage with its surrounding entrenchments, and the church tower at the back. The exact date I am unable to give, but it is here reproduced.

Once some mischievous rogue, after liberally treating the sentinel to something stronger than water, got at the bell in the "*wee sma' hours ayont the twal*" in a dark and rainy night. He rang the appointed signal and alarmed the town. The officer in charge sent his men round to prevent a general rush to the Griqua Church. Somehow *Mrs. Brownlee*, who had no one with her that night except a policeman to keep watch, and *Mrs Grierson*, a lady of high degree, who had shortly before become a mother, received no notice. The two ladies, carrying Mrs. Grierson's child and bedding, struggled through the darkness, rain and mud to the place of *rendezvous*. There they slept for the night.

The cost of living became serious because of the difficulty of transport The season was exceptionally wet, and the unbridged rivers continued in flood. To meet this difficulty resort was had to *barrel punts*. Empty barrels were securely fixed to transverse beams. These were planked over, and the whole thing floated and held in position by a strong rope stretched from side to side. On these a loaded wagon could be floated over, while the oxen swam through. The position of these barrel punts was a little below the site of the present Turbine Mill, and they did excellent service in a sore strait. The mechanism was not quite perfect. The writer and his wife set out one afternoon to visit *Mr. and Mrs. Usher*, who, after the death of their son, needed and deserved all sympathy and attention We got through all right, swimming the horses at the back of the punt, but on returning, in the gloaming, the pulley got entangled, and there we stuck in mid stream, while darkness came on. By a desperate final effort, not unattended with danger, I succeeded in righting the gearing and getting through, just as the return of the horses to their stables alarmed the household.

After the stress and strain and danger of the first month was over, things settled down a bit. Kokstad put on the appearance of a garrison town. Commissariat, Ordinance, Pay, Intelligence and other officers occupied every shed and shanty in the place, at excessive rents. The Bank had an army of clerks ; specie came up by every mail cart ; storekeepers were doing a lucrative business ; looted cattle came in by hundreds and were sold ; remount horses came in in droves ; hotels, canteens and billiard-rooms were always crowded, and often became the scene of hilarity and miserable strife. Altogether, the little town became a focus of military officialism and the centre of incredable commercial activity. Many thousands of pounds were brought into circulation every week. Fuel became scarce and very dear. Packing box wood was sold at 2½d a lb. I remember well paying 7s. 6d. for sufficient fuel for cooking from Saturday till Monday. Living, without getting into debt, became a very serious difficulty At the end of three weeks after the outbreak I had no more *officers pay* or official status, and so had no *orderly* to dance attendance as most others had. Nearly every white man was an *officer*, commandant, captain, adjutant, or something of the sort, and each had his orderly to do the rough work.

At this time my printing press proved of great service to the public, and to myself also in helping to keep the "wolf from the door." I brought the press with me from Britain in 1878, and had set it up in an outside room, "*the printing office*." I had acquired sufficient knowledge of the printer's art to be able to do such work as was required in connection with church and school. Now it proved quite a Godsend. My daughter often filled the place of printer's devil. The press is now, or was, part of the plant of the *Kokstad Advertiser*. I printed, bound, and perforated thousands of *Bank Cheque Forms*, and occasionally regimental returns and such like, and right thankful I was of the chance to earn something extra to meet the advanced cost of living.

Servants' wages became almost unpayable. At 5s a day it was difficult, sometimes impossible, to get a boy to milk cows and clean shoes. I remember one Sunday morning being in sore straits. The cows had to be milked, and there was no one to do it. Necessity has no law. Ministers and their families are hungry mortals. Leaving the study and the sermon, I betook myself to the cowshed, milk-pail in hand, and made a start. Things went prosperously enough at first, and I was becoming confident, feeling independent of all domestic help, when "*Houtskool*" lost her temper, and sent minister and milkpail bang against the wall, pretty well ruining his suit of "blacks," bruising his bones, humbling his pride, and producing a state of feeling and temper not suited to the sacred work of the day I had used to think, and even boast (may I be forgiven), that I could do anything of a mechanical nature which any other man could do. Since that day, if ever I venture, in an evil moment, to forget that boasting is excluded, I am asked by some member of my family, "How about milking, father?" "Mum" is the word. "Let us change the subject."

Mr. Liefeldt, Magistrate of Matatiela, left Moteri's Kop on the night when Makwai and his people crossed the *Rubicon*, and rose in rebellion. Liefeldt left his home as it stood, taking only horse saddle and saddle-bag—or rather, the horse took him and them. The Basutos spoiled his well-appointed bachelor's quarters. He had a new and excellent "*spider*." They, the Basutos, would have a turn of the white man's luxury, why not? They yoked to the spider a pair of wild oxen, and went careering over the veldt. A mist hung on the land. Brandy from the plundered stores had mystified the revellers. The oxen, left to their own sweet will, landed the equipage on the edge of a krantz, the spider capsized and stuck fast The oxen wrenched off the pole and left the spider sticking there. Months thereafter a wagoner returning empty from one of the camps, hitched on his team, tore the spider from its moorings, loaded it up, and brought it to Kokstad. There he tried to sell it, but could get no offer, and left it on the edge of the highway. There it lay for a year and a half. A certain gentleman not unknown to the writer, tried to buy it, but no one would own proprietorship. Liefeldt said, "I claim compensation from Government for a *new spider*, if I sell I damage my claim." Brownlee said, "Liefeldt claims compensation, if I sell for Government, I commit Government to the full payment of his claim." Each said, "you may have the wreck for the taking for all I care." And so this gentleman jumped the wreck of the disowned carriage, got its crooked irons straightened out, and with his own hands "did it up." For years he used it as a "*gospel chariot*" and a family conveyance. I knew that man eighteen years ago, I know him still, but I am not to mention his name. "Silence is sometimes golden" I mention this as one of the many humorous side incidents of the war.

Here is another :—One night Mr. Brownlee sat late in his office writing for the out-going mail. He had forgotten to get the "pass-word." On his way home he was challenged, and could not give it.

"*Oh, but you know me, surely. Don't you?*"

"Sir, my orders are to bring to the guard room whoever fails to give the pass-word. You must come with me."

"*All right! Go on!*"

Arrived at the guard-room, Brownlee said :—"*This man has run me in, because I haven't the pass-word.*"

"Why did you not tell him your name, sir?"

"*But the man knows me quite well.*"

"That may be, but 'Brownlee' is the pass-word. I'll send him to see you home."

And they all enjoyed the humour of the incident.

After long weary months of waiting and sometimes privation, at last the war terminated. The Kafirs returned to their homes with accumulated pay in their pockets. The European regiments, "*Baker's Horse*" and "*Willoughby's Horse*," were disbanded Willoughby went from Kokstad to Madagascar to worm himself into the good books of the Prime Minister and

Queen, and became Envoy Extraordinary from the Malagasy Government to that of France, trained the Malagasy soldiers, and led them in the war with France, and thereafter was dismissed from his post as a discredited adventurer.

The farmers all returned to their farms. Many found their homes wantonly destroyed. The Basutos did not burn down the houses, but they smashed the furniture to pieces, ripped up the mattrasses and pillows, and scattered the contents ruthlessly about in search of cash. The destruction by fire was chiefly the work of *our own troops*. So keenly did many of the farmers feel this that some declared that the protectors were more to be feared than the invaders.

The traders were the chief sufferers. Nearly every store was destroyed. All that could be eaten or drunk or worn the Basutos took possession of. All that would burn the troops consumed. Between them they left behind a desert. Neither traders nor farmers received compensation. The hardest part of this was when the farmers could distinguish their own stock among the captured herds, and identify their registered mark, yet could not recover it. My readers will easily understand the heartburnings which would arise from the enforcement of the rule which made recovery impossible. We must not altogether blame those in authority, seeing that any other course would have opened the door for grave and serious irregularities.

The Basutos, who had rebelled, were now out of Griqualand East, and in Basutoland. The lands they had occupied were the lands which the Griquas considered ought to have been kept in reserve for their benefit. The circumstance of their being now empty re-opened the old question. There was a recurrence to the old crop of "*vergaderings*," speeches, petitions, &c , but without result The Basutos had forfeited their lands, and the Government naturally claimed them, and the sole right of their disposal.

With the termination of the Basuto War ends what may be fitly called the *Early Annals* of the Town and District. For, about this time, the *Kokstad Advertiser* was started, and it has continued, without a break, to record current public events. The establishment of such a newspaper marks the coming of age of a township. I shall therefore close these Early Annals by a brief statement of facts, probably not generally known to the present residents, as to the origin of the paper and the two men who were chief actors in it, and well known characters in their time. The originator of the paper was a coloured man and an American, familiarly known as "*Yankee Wood*." He had conducted Hotels in various towns in the Colony, and acquired quite an exceptional agility and "*slimness*" in working his way through the Bankruptcy Court If these freaks of fortune had made gaps in his honour, he wore, nevertheless, his errors like a crown. He could start new enterprises requiring considerable capital, with marvellous facility. He came to Kokstad in 1878, and began his new career there by buying a farm and building the Royal Hotel, the first double-storied house in the place. Then he opened business as Hotel-keeper. In a short time he built Tabernacle Row, and let all the shops in it. Then he talked Captain Blyth over to allow him to open a canteen, and though well stricken in years, he took a very young local girl to wife. Waxing bold, and determined to show what a coloured man of public spirit could do, he imported printing plant and a printer to start a weekly paper. But how about an Editor? "Yankee" honoured (?) the writer by offering him the Editor's chair, with the off chance of emoluments coming by-and-by. Declined with thanks! Among Yankee's best customers was a Scotch gentleman of broken means, and given to starts and bursts of revel. He had worn the wig and gown of an Advocate in Parliament House, Edinburgh. He had been clothed with the official dignity and the robes of Town Clerk to an ancient Scottish borough. But disgraces had knocked at his door. He had found it advisable to leave Scotland, and had found his way to out of the way Kokstad. He had practised in the local Court, had answered a serious charge, and had worn the broad arrow with the air of a martyr. He was well read, had the gift of eloquence, could speak and write on any subject—almost an ideal Editor—just the man! Here then was an American with go, mysterious capital, good plant, ample material, printer stick in hand and heaps of copy. And so No. 1 of the *Kokstad Advertiser* saw the light. It was by prophetic instinct it was called "*Advertiser*." I question if the first numbers had a single paying Advertisement. The very first copy was handed to me while presiding at a Griqua Tea Meeting. It has continued to appear weekly without a break, recording local events, obviating the necessity for my continuing the recital of Kokstad History from that date.

I will only enumerate the more important events which transpired in *Griqualand East* after the termination of the Basuto War.

These were:—The visit of General Gordon of Chinese and Egyptian fame; the commencement of the *Kokstad Advertiser*; the advent of the *Cape Infantry Regiment*; the erection of the *Roman Catholic Church*; the outbreak of public feeling at the establishment of a Custom House at Umzimkulu; the opening of the road to St. John's; the retirement of Mr. Brownlee and appointment of Mr. Stanford to the Chief Magistracy; the first visit of a Judge in the person of Mr. *Justice Maasdorp*, and the sitting of the first Circuit Court; the celebration of the Queen's Jubilee; the establishment of the Public School, the Agricultural Society, the Public Library, the

Municipality; the election of James Sivewright, Esq., to be the first representative of the district to Parliament; the visit of Sir Henry Loch; the erection of the Prison, the Bridge and the Public Offices; the erection of the Hospital with its Memorial Tablet, to Commandant H. Usher: the mad escapades of Le Fluer. All these things behold are they not written in the book of the Chronicles of the district, which is the *Kokstad Advertiser*.

APPENDIX.

Le Fleur, the Forty Years' Money, and the Rising of 1897.

Abraham Le Fleur was known to all the residents of Kokstad as a confirmed grievance-monger. To agitate for the redress of some grievance, real or imaginary, in Church or State, had become to this man almost as natural and instinctive as it is for a dog to bark or a fish to swim. And yet he took no part in the attempted revolts in 1896-97. Why? Perhaps the following statement may throw some light on this question, which has puzzled more than one.

During the years between 1870 and 1884 I had become pretty well used to the incessant and somewhat pointless complaints about the "*Forty Years Money*." Nobody could give me any intelligible statement of the facts of the case, or of the grounds of complaint. I had access to no records, and had little time to devote to the subject.

The public excitement created by annexation in 1874, and continued during the Basuto War, was not favourable to research. The resumption of the regular annual distribution of the moneys coming to the participants, and especially the payment to them of what had fallen in arrear under the old Government, had resulted in comparative satisfaction and contentment. Less was heard now of the *Forty Years' Money*, and expressions of thankfulness were common, when the yearly dole came round.

All this was changed on the arrival of Le Fluer about 1884. His pretended knowledge of all the facts, and his manifestly extravagant statements served to create a spirit of expectancy, which was destructive to all my efforts in trying to urge the poor people to that persevering industry which I firmly believed to be their only salvation from utter extinction as a tribe. As the result of this man's senseless vapourings, there was created a common belief that forty years after the date of the *Smith Treaty*, (that is in 1888), the Griquas would either recover the possession of hundreds of farms in the O.F.S., approximately three millions of acres, or the Imperial Government would have to compensate for the loss of these. There was not a family amongst them but would directly or indirectly become entitled to some share.

Determined to get at the bottom of this somewhat tangled and mysterious subject, I availed myself of a visit to Cape Town to consult the public and press records of the period. Mr. Brisley also allowed me the use of a quantity of old Griqua Government papers bearing on the subject.

After several months of laborious research, I reached the following conclusions:—

(1). That, while there is indisputable evidence of gross injustice and high-handed spoilation, it is now practically impossible to fix or to apportion the responsibility and blame in each respective case.

(2). That, even if that could be done, there is no competent tribunal to which a formal appeal could be made, unless all parties concerned, including the owners of the farms, should consent, and bind themselve to the principle of *arbitration*, which is in the last degree improbable.

(3). That even if the most sanguine expectations of the Griquas, in this matter, could be realised, either by *retrocession* or *compensation*, a new and even greater difficulty would arise in effecting a strictly just distribution of the land, or the proceeds, among the hosts which would arise to claim a share. Unfortunately, all church registers of marriages, births and baptisms up to 1861 have disappearedf In very rare instances were family registers kept, and o Government registration there was none. Hence, it would be almost impossible to produce the legal evidence required to deal with such cases even with approximate accuracy.

Thus I was compelled to occupy the unenviable position of being a messenger of evil tidings to the expectant people, in fact, dashing in pieces the only faint remaining hope of an easy return to former prosperity. Le Fleur did not share my views. He preached persistently his crusade of *Retrocession* or *Compensation*. He vaguely hinted that I, being a white man—would naturally take the view favouring the white man. He advocated no abatement or abandonment of their claims, he urged united and firm action, even to the extent of an appeal to the Queen herself by a Griqua deputation, and, all else failing, occasionally hinted at the display of force.

Finding that nothing could be accomplished regarding these lapsed farms, I turned my attention to the various questions arising out of the provisions of the *Smith Treaty*. Here the objective seemed more definite and attainable.

It must be understood that the Griquas usually confuse these two separate cases—the *lapsed farms* and the *annual payment*, and with their usual lack of accuracy, call both under the common designation of the *Forty Years Money*.

I began by endeavouring to construct correct lists, first of the *original* 42 participants under the Smith Treaty; second, of those still *alive*; and third, of the heirs of those *deceased*. This required much labour, time and travel. I venture to say that the lists thus made out and supplied to the Government and to the people were approximately correct. Absolute accuracy is impossible.

The practical outcome was that immediately thereafter some four hundred pounds of arrears was distributed amongst heirs scattered over the whole of South Africa.

Then I vainly tried to persuade Government to make the whole £300 payable to the original owners of the farms and their heirs, on the death of the chief's wife. Beyond all doubt, the spirit and history of the original transaction justified this proposal, but the *letter* of the Treaty was against it.

Failing in that, I urged Government to *capitalise* on the basis of ten or twelve years' payment, to distribute the money and to let the whole business end.

Failing in that, I again urged the Government to capitalise and deal with the fund *tribally* and to administer it for the *General Good*, by the *endowment* of churches and schools, or by the establishment of a *Loan Fund* to encourage Griqua industry by cheap advances on security, or by some similar scheme.

In discussing these various proposals, I met with the hearty sympathy of the Chief Magistrate, *W. Stanford, Esq.*, of the *Honourable J. Rose-Innes*, of the Native Affairs Department, of *Sir James Sivewright*, the member for Griqualand East, and of the Attorney-General and Premier at the time, *Sir T. Upington*.

In the opinion of the last named, the legal difficulties, in the way of all these proposals, were quite insuperable, and the prospect of obtaining Parliamentary sanction so very slight, that Government would not take the responsibility of asking for it.

The present position is that £100 is annually voted by Parliament; that an annually decreasing portion is distributed amongst the heirs; and an annually increasing portion remains unpaid Ultimately the payment must lapse altogether, although declared to be "*in perpetuity*."

Le Fleur continued to stir the blood of the people by his wild, extravagant statements, not lacking in veiled threats and hostile insinuations. Most of the people had sold their lands, spent the proceeds and were, Macauber-like, "waiting for something to turn up," or, as they gracefully put it in the Taal, "*Ik leef bij planne*" (I live by my wits). My persistent advice was this: "You have nothing to expect from "the O.F.S. farms, you have wasted your substance here, "now off with your coats, one and all of you, old and young, "and go to work every day, thus only can you save your-"selves from starvation or beggary." All my admonitions and my example were wasted in the presence of a slim demagogue of their own colour, who spoke with confidence about *compelling* Government to restore or compensate. It is so much easier to sit down and cry for the moon than to dig in the garden. The poor people have long ere now discovered, however, that this is hungry work, leaves its mark upon them, and gives them as the burden of their daily song the somewhat lugubrious ditty: "*My leanness, my leanness.*"

All this was vexatious enough, and ultimately drove me to an expedient I was loath to adopt, but it was my last shot in the locker for Le Fleur.

In my researches among old Griqua documents I had found a *Warrant for the Apprehension* of one A. Le Fleur, on a charge of horse-stealing, signed by the Magistrate of Colesberg, and dated as far back as 1850. This document was in my possession. I decided to use it "*in terrorem.*" One day I invited Le Fleur to my study, and reasoned with him as to the folly and mischief of his conduct. He stuck to his guns, repeating all his arguments. Then I produced the Warrant, and ventured on the assertion that the Writ of a British Magistrate did not lose its force by lapse of time. "Le Fleur," I said, "if you persist in "keeping up this mischievous agitation which is ruining "the people, I shall deem it my duty to place this document "in the hands of the law officers. Take care!" The agitation ceased, and there was peace and quietness till after my departure from Kokstad in 1890.

Thereafter Andries Le Fleur, the son, took up his father's old song, and renewed the agitation. He had married the daughter of the late *Adam Muis Kok*, the quondam expectant of Kok's captaincy, and the leader of the revolt of 1878. He, Le Fleur, claimed now to be the *representative* of the Kok family and to sit in the old chief's seat. He affected to ignore the fact of annexation, he talked incessantly of retrocession, he assumed the role of the martyr, held a court, sent to and received messages from petty chiefs in the territory, and generally created a political ferment. The father had been bad enough, the son was worse. The father contented himself with words, speeches, despatches, protests, memorials, lectures, threats; the son prepared for action. His wife had no sympathy with his visionary schemes. She was quiet, hard-working respectable, without any ambitious projects. He suffered grievously from head-swelling.

In some mysterious way young Le Fleur managed to persuade the Griquas and Kafirs to provide him with funds. He turned up in Cape Town in July, 1894, while Rev. Mr. Murray and I were there together. He assumed wonderful airs, and his pockets were crammed with Bluebooks and official-looking documents. He condescended to speak with us on the street, but handed us his card, and politely hinted that we would find thereon his address and reception hours. I met him subsequently, by accident, in the Native Affairs Office, and heard him receive a severe reprimand for daring to address insulting despatches to H. E. the High Commissioner, despatches containing manifest untruths, gross exaggerations, and generally distinguished by ambiguity and cheek. Our gentleman went off in high dungeon "to appeal "to the Colonial Secretary in London and, *if need be, to the "Queen herself*, for that justice denied to her subjects by her "servants in South Africa." But instead of going to London by the first steamer he returned to Kokstad. There he organised two unsuccessful revolts, and returned to Cape Town under sentence of 15 years' hard labour. His case is a striking illustration of the old saying, "The Gods first madden those they mean to destroy."

The circumstance of the *Warrant of Apprehension* had passed out of my mind until the following took place here in Port Elizabeth. Sometime before Le Fleur's outbreak I found the elder Le Fleur one morning in my study. He had come from Kokstad, and now sought the address of certain friends. He was on his way to Capetown "*to "deliver a series of Lectures on the relations of coloured to white "citizens and specifically to educate public opinion as to Griqua "claims on the Imperial and Colonial Governments*" I never heard a word of the *Lectures*, but some weeks thereafter

Le Fleur appeared at my usual Sunday evening service. He asked and received permission to remain for Communion. In my congregation there is an old deacon, *Christian Davids*. He is held in high respect for his piety and long service. When he was a young man he was groom to the late Hess, Esq. He was a trusted servant, and had charge of a valuable horse. His fellow-servant was *Abraham Le Fleur*, One morning Christian awoke to find man and horse gone. Both were traced to Colesberg, and the warrant for his arrest followed. The two had never again met till that night. It fell to *Christian* to hand the sacred symbols to this man who had caused him years of sorrow and nearly ruined his character. Very affecting was the mental struggle and distress the good old man passed through before he could bring himself to pass the elements to Le Fleur. Charity triumphed.

Le Fleur promised to come next day and describe his doings in Cape Town and give me an account of the Lectures. But next day he had disappeared, leaving no trace.

Perhaps the people of Griqualand East will now better understand why the father lay low while the son was at his wild goose chase.

APPENDIX NO. II

In accordance with the expressed wish of friends, I have added the following to the character sketches to be found on preceding pages.

Abraham Jantjes.

This man was, physically, as pure a Griqua as lived. He was one of the few left who could speak the old Hottentot language. He was a distinct exception from the ordinary run of Griquas, in three particulars:—1st, He was by no means afraid of hard work; 2nd, He had a wholesome dread of evil-doing in every form; 3rd, He tried to honour the Divine command, "Owe no man anything but to love one another." Abraham was a Christian man, and a useful, active Church officer. Although he had more brain power than any man in the tribe, he was quite unconscious of it; he was and remained humble and simple as a very child. He declined to accept of any office under the Griqua Government. It was an unwritten law that no one should, simultaneously, hold office in Church and State. Abraham believed that he had to serve his fellowmen, in connection with Church life, and he made no small sacrifices to his convictions of duty.

He was the *dramatist* of the tribe—a born actor every inch of him. Even in private conversation, on any supject which affected him, the art of the actor shewed itself. But when he spoke publicly, which he did only in connection with church life and work, and when he was moved by strong conviction or inward passion, he let himself fairly go, and then, what he said and how he said it, left an impression on the hearer never to be effaced. Of course, one required to have a pretty intimate acquaintance with the "taal," or the colloquial Dutch usually spoken among the Griquas, in order to catch the subtle wit, the histrionic force, the indescribable aroma of what he said on these occasions. Unlike most Griqua speakers, he only spoke when he had something to say, and was all aflame to say it. Then the little grey eyes shone, and the dark, coarse, rugged features changed with the varying moods, and every motion of head and hand served to depict the passion which animated him. He could tell a simple incident in his experience, as, for instance, his first and only sight of a railway train, with such graphic language and dramatic action, that one felt transported into the surroundings he described, to be an eyewitness, and share his surprise or indignation, his gladness or sorrow. More than any native man I have ever met, he possessed the subtle power of infecting his hearers with his own passion.

At a Griqua Tea Meeting Abraham was at his best, if there happened to be no other Europeans present except myself or any other members of the mission family or staff. If other Europeans, especially strangers, were present, he was shy and reserved, refused to be drawn, cut his speech short, and begged to be excused, because "*he was no speaker*."

If the old man was still alive, and I had the chance, I would walk a good many miles to hear him describing again his first sight of a wagon, "a house on wheels," or to hear him give a pharaphrase of some of the New Testament parables or of the Old Testament histories. These he could clothe in the garb of everyday Griqua life, and make the actors pass before you like living men, very much in the style adopted by the famous Welsh preacher, Christmass Evans.

I venture to reproduce one of Abraham's stories, but I am quite unable to put into it the aroma of humour with which he could tell it.

"When I was a little fellow, not much taller than this "walking-stick, I could shoot birds with my home-made bow "and arrow. I could swim in the reaches of the Vaal River, "catch eels in its muddy holes, gather blink klippies "(diamonds) and play with them, or ride on a calf, with any "Griqua boy of my age; but I had never seen a book, or "been inside a school or church, or seen a white man. One "day my father told me I was to go to *Klaarwater*, now "Griquatown, to school. That night I nearly cried my eyes "out. I was terrified at the thought of seeing a white man. "I had heard the grown-up men tell dreadful stories round "the camp fires of the doings of the white man. After a "long ride on oxback we came to the Mission Station. O "dear!! how big the houses looked, and how white, and "what huge doors, and how strange to stand inside and look "out and yet to find that there was some hard substance "between you and the clear air, and oh! those 'houses on "wheels.' I crept cautiously up to where I could see the "white man's house, in the hope that I might see himself. "I had heard the grown-up people always say that all white "men had a peculiar odour, and that you could feel it a "good distance off, so I looked and snuffed up the "wind, but could feel nothing, see nobody. Next day I was "taken to the school, and felt frightened when I took my "seat and my father went away and left me. The school "house had been newly painted, and the smell of the paint "was particularly strong and offensive to me. As I was "wondering whence came this strange smell, the white man "came in, and I said to myself, 'Yes, it is quite true, the "white man does smell strong.' It was a long time before "I outgrew that childish impression, and even now the smell "of paint recalls my first sight of a white man."

Abraham was selected by Captain Blyth to make a final appeal to the insurgents, on the slopes of Mount Currie, on the morning of the fight, 1878. He took his life in his hand and he went. He pleaded with them as only he could plead. In vain; they abused him, threatened him, and he barely escaped with his life. Captain Blyth knew that, if they wouldn't listen to Abraham, there was nothing left but to fight.

Abraham lived on a few years after I left Kokstad. He had been fleeced by relatives who took advantage of his generosity. He became poor, but stuck to a considerable part of his farm. He died peacefully, and left an unblemished mame and a kindly memory behind him.

METJE JOOD.—A widow, indeed, of many years' standing. She was born somewhere in the interior, but was brought to *Bethelsdorp* early in the century. There she was trained as a Teacher. She remembered seeing Dr. Van der Kemp baptising converts in the streamlet running through the village. Metje taught the first school which was opened in this town of Port Elizabeth about the date of the arrival of the settlers, 1820. The house in which this school was held is one of the oldest structures in the town, and now forms the kitchen to the Manse in which these Annals are being compiled. There are men alive to-day who have taken no inconsiderable part in the commercial and public life of South Africa who learned their alphabet in Metje's school.

She married into the Griqua *Jood* family, and was left a widow with two children. She crossed the Drakensberg in the Trek, and settled in the new country. She maintained herself by her own industry. She could turn her hand to almost anything. She was certainly the most advanced in intelligence and general knowledge of all the Griqua women. Her piety was sincere and practical. She was full of good works. She was trusted and respected by all who knew her as a worthy, consistent Christian woman.

FLAT was an obscure Hottentot man of the purest breed. He was originally from the Kat River Settlement. I found him in the old Laager when I came there. I had ample opportunity of studying this man's character and ways. My curiosity was excited by noting that the man had no visible means of subsistence. He had no money or stock, he had no field or garden, did no work, but sat all day in the sun discussing the latest case in the Magistrate's Court, the doings of the *Volksraad*, or the wild schemes of the new minister. There was always smoke in his chimney, but no one ever saw him fetch fuel. His wife stamped mealies daily, but he neither grew them nor bought them, nor, so far as I could find out, earned them. Whence came this fuel and food? When I put this question to any of the more respectable Griquas, up went the shoulders and out went the spread-out palms, which is in Griqua dumb-show-language as much as saying, "*I don't know.*" I found that every evening after dark *Flat* set out with a stick in his hand and a haversack on his back. On several occasions duty called me to be astir at an early hour, and I caught sight of *Flat* coming home, somewhat stealthily, with the haversack evidently *not empty*. This went on for some time, and I formed my own conclusions, which I found confirmed by the general opinion expressed in the common verdict, "*Flat is slim.*"

Now, *Flat* was one of the most violent opponents to the removal of the township. He was amendable to no reason, and left no stone unturned to thwart my plans. One day I quietly asked him where he went so mysteriously every night with the haversack, and what it contained when he returned in the early morning. "You know, *Flat*, it may be all quite right, but it looks bad, now, doesn't it?" Flat's opposition died out.

Sometime after the bulk of the people had moved into the new township Flat reluctantly followed suit, and I have reason to believe that the old practice continued. But one day, to my surprise, I found *Flat* among my penitents—a candidate for church membership, "*wanting to be a Christian*" In dealing with the man I felt constrained to say to him something like this:—"Flat, if you are to "become a Christian, you must be done with all works of "darkness, you must be in your bed like an honest man at "night, and not prowling about all over the country rousing "suspicion and giving the appearance of evil. I will believe "in the sincerity of your profession when you burn that old "haversack, become possessed of a spade, and set about "digging in your own garden, growing your own mealies "and eating them." *Flat* got rid of the haversack, slept at home at night, and, after a period of probation, became a member of the church. He has never made any very high attainments in Christian life or character, but the old suspicious ways have been abandoned. He has a spade, but I am afraid the use of it has not been a distinguished success. He prefers hanging about the shops to hold the horse of a customer. He could go a message even for miles with incredible rapidity, and thus it is that he kept hunger at bay.

During my recent visit to Kokstad I found *Flat* in his old post. I was guilty of the incivility of greeting my old friend with *gloved hands.* His greeting seemed to lack cordiality, and the following conversation brought out the reason. It illustrates a phase of character by no means uncommon even amongst the poorest of the tribe.

"*Sir, may I be allowed to ask you one question?* O, Cer-"tainly, *Flat. Well, my question is, When the Christ was here "on earth, do you think He would have greeted any of his "disciples with gloved hands?* Well, Flat, I think that gloves "were probably very scarce in those days. *Yes, very likely.*

WAGON HOUSE.—The first building erected in Kokstad.

KOKSTAD TOWN HALL.

Lightning Source UK Ltd.
Milton Keynes UK
UKHW012118200121
377399UK00004B/1030

9 789353 609139